THE CANTEEN

Sacrifice and Community during World War II

Published by Arcadia Children's Books
A Division of Arcadia Publishing
Charleston, SC
www.arcadiapublishing.com

First published 2022

Designed by Jessica Nevins, John Craft, and Eric Groce

Manufactured in the United States

ISBN 978-1-4671-9707-6

Library of Congress Control Number: 2022940319

Notice: The information in this book is true and complete to the best of our knowledge. It is offered without guarantee on the part of the author or Arcadia Publishing. The author and Arcadia Publishing disclaim all liability in connection with the use of this book.

We would like to thank the following individuals and organizations for providing images:

North Platte Public Library
Lincoln County Historical Museum (North Platte, NE)
National Archives and Records Administration
Library of Congress
B&O Railroad Museum
Union Pacific Railroad Museum
Dr. John Craft
University of North Texas Libraries' World War Poster Collection
World War II Poster Collection at Northwestern University Library
Ann Milton
Brenda Purswell
Debbie Dowden
Darla Bayless
Rosalie Lippincott
St. Patrick's Catholic Church (North Platte, NE)
Episcopal Church of Our Savior (North Platte, NE)
Black Watch Museum; Balhousie Castle Perth, Scotland
Nebraska National Guard Museum
Steve Kay

THE CANTEEN

Sacrifice and Community during World War II

Eric Groce

arcadia®
CHILDREN'S BOOKS

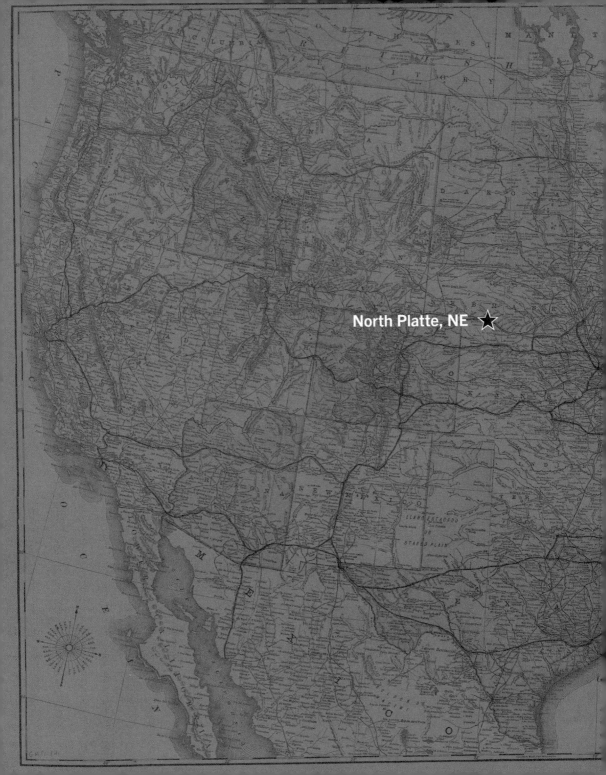

North Platte, NE ★

This book is dedicated to the resolute and gracious women of North Platte and surrounding communities who started and sustained the Canteen through a difficult chapter in American history.

May their dedication and spirit be an example to all of us.

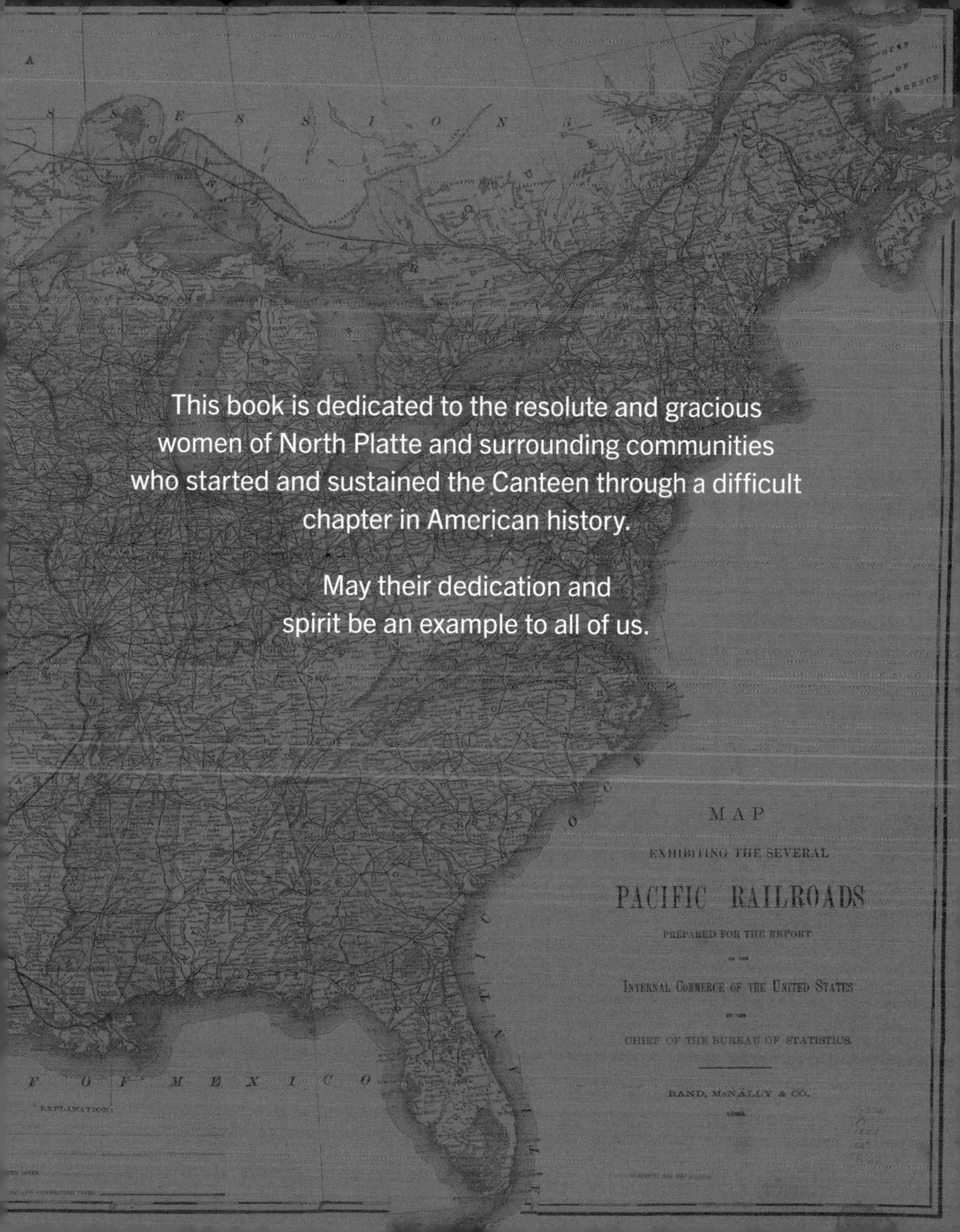

MAP

EXHIBITING THE SEVERAL

PACIFIC RAILROADS

PREPARED FOR THE REPORT

ON THE

INTERNAL COMMERCE OF THE UNITED STATES

BY THE

CHIEF OF THE BUREAU OF STATISTICS.

RAND, McNALLY & CO.

Pearl Harbor 1941

On December 7, 1941, Japanese forces bombed the US naval base at Pearl Harbor, Hawaii. The attack decimated the fleet, including 18 warships and over 160 aircraft. More than 2,400 American soldiers, sailors, and civilians died in the attack. Until that moment, the US had stayed out of World War II, which had been raging since 1939. But now the enemy had come to our shores, and America was drawn into the war. In his famous speech to Congress, President Franklin D. Roosevelt said the December 7th attack was a "premeditated invasion" and a "date which will live in infamy." A day later, he prepared the nation for the long road ahead during a fireside chat. "We are now in this war. We are all in it all the way. Every single man, woman, and child is a partner in the most tremendous undertaking of our American history."

While the attack on Pearl Harbor was a surprise, world leaders had been closely watching what was happening in Europe as Germany invaded Poland, Czechoslovakia, France, and Russia. Starting in 1940, the US military had been recruiting soldiers so that if we did have to enter the war, we'd be prepared. In the days and weeks following our entry into World War II, hundreds of thousands of young men from around the country entered military service to do their part. The women and children left at home did the same—banding together to support the troops, their families, their communities, and the nation. Over the course of the war, one community in particular made a lasting impact on countless Americans: the people of North Platte, Nebraska. This is the story of their herculean efforts to bring warmth and cheer to millions of soldiers.

Troop movement was classified information, but the news had leaked and was spreading like a prairie fire through North Platte that many of the local boys would be coming through town. The steam locomotive was scheduled to stop for just ten minutes to fill the tender rail car with water and lubricate the wheels. Five hundred people stood in the biting December winds with Christmas gifts and homemade treats to share with Nebraska National Guard Company D as they headed toward the fight for freedom.

TO THE CONGRES

Yest

live in infamy

and deliberat

Empire of Japa

The

at the solicit

its Government

of peace in th

squadrons had

sador to the U

Secretary of S

While this rep

existing diplo

hint of war or

It w

F THE UNITED STATES:

y, December 7, 1941 — a d

the United States of Amer

attacked by naval

ed

n c

it

cifi

ence

d Sta

e a formal reply to a recen

tated that it seemed usel

o negotiations, it contain

d attack.

be recorded that the distance of Hawaii from

The train, already running a few hours late, finally arrived around 5:00 p.m. As the giant wheels finally came to rest, mothers, fathers, and sweethearts pushed against the train, searching for familiar faces, but no one on that troop train called North Platte home. The servicemen aboard were from National Guard Company D . . . in Kansas.

During the era of steam-powered locomotives, North Platte served as a service stop along the route. During the brief ten-minute stop, Union Pacific employees rushed to re lubricate the giant wheels and refill the tender car with water and coal.

The March 1943 Union Pacific Overland Route train schedule, which covered the Chicago to Los Angeles route, including a stop in North Platte using the 4-6-6-4 Challenger locomotive.

The *Challenger* Between CHICAGO, OMAHA and LOS ANGELES

Miles	PLACE		Chicago to Los Angeles (Read Down)	Los Angeles to Chicago (Read Up)
			No. 7	*No. 8*
	C. & N. W.			
0	**CHICAGO**......(Central Time).....Ill.	Lv.	8:30 PM	Ar. 9:00 AM
485	Council Bluffs................Iowa	Ar.	7:35 AM	Lv. 10:15 PM
488	Omaha....................Neb.	Ar.	8:00 AM	Lv. 10:00 PM
	Union Pacific			
488	**OMAHA**..................Neb.	Lv.	8:45 AM	Ar. 9:30 PM
525	Fremont...................."	Lv.f	9:37 AM	Lv. 8:30 PM
570	Columbus..................."	Lv.	10:34 AM	Lv. 7:36 PM
632	Grand Island..............."	Lv.	12:05 PM	Lv. 6:20 PM
674	Kearney (State Normal)......."	Lv.	1:00 PM	Lv. 5:04 PM
769	North Platte (Central Time)...."	Ar.	2:55 PM	Lv. 3:15 PM
769	North Platte (Mountain Time).."	Lv.	2:03 PM	Ar. 2:05 PM
893	Sidney...................."	Lv.	5:01 PM	Lv. 11:40 AM
995	Cheyenne (Capital of Wyoming).Wyo.	Ar.	7:45 PM	Lv. 9:45 AM
995	Cheyenne (Fort Warren)......"	Lv.	8:55 PM	Ar. 9:15 AM
1051	Laramie (State University)....."	Ar.	10:35 PM	Lv. 7:35 AM
1051	Laramie (Snowy Range to West).."	Lv.	10:45 PM	Ar. 7:20 AM
1168	Rawlins (State Penitentiary)...."	Lv.	1:35 AM	Lv. 4:35 AM
1287	Rock Springs (Coal Mines)....."	Lv.	4:04 AM	Lv. 1:42 AM
1302	Green River (Water flows to Gulf	Ar.	4:30 AM	Lv. 1:20 AM
1302	Green River of California)...."	Lv.	4:50 AM	Ar. 12:55 AM
1402	Evanston..................."	Lv.	7:20 AM	Lv. 10:40 PM
1478	Ogden (Junction with So. Pac.)..Utah	Ar.	9:30 AM	Ar. 8:40 PM
1478	Ogden...................."	Lv.	10:10 AM	Ar. 8:10 PM
1514	Salt Lake City (State Capital).."	Ar.	11:15 AM	Lv. 7:00 PM
0	St. Louis (Wabash)...........Mo.	Lv.	3:50 PM	Ar. 3:00 PM
278	Kansas City (U. P.)..........."	Lv.	11:30 PM	Lv. 2:10 PM
918	Denver....................Colo.	Lv.	4:40 PM	Lv. 1:00 PM
1531	Salt Lake City..............Utah	Ar.	9:30 AM	Lv. 7:00 PM
1514	Salt Lake City.............."	Lv.	11:55 AM	Ar. 6:30 PM
1632	Lynndyl..................."	Lv.	3:30 PM	Lv. 3:15 PM
1649	Delta...................."	Lv.	4:05 PM	Lv.f 2:35 PM
1721	Milford (To Lehman's Cave)...."	Lv.	6:15 PM	Lv. 1:05 PM
1757	Lund (Gateway Utah-Ariz. Parks)"	Lv.	7:05 PM	Lv. 12:04 PM
1839	Caliente (Mountain Time).....Nev.	Ar.	9:20 PM	Lv. 9:55 AM
1839	Caliente (Pacific Time)......."	Lv.	8:35 PM	Ar. 8:35 AM
1964	Las Vegas................."	Ar.	11:59 PM	Lv. 5:20 AM
1964	Las Vegas................."	Lv.	12:20 AM	Ar. 5:00 AM
2063	Kelso (Death Valley Divide)...Cal.	Lv.	3:30 AM	Lv. 2:13 AM
2135	Yermo Mojave River and...Cal.	Lv.	5:50 AM	Lv. 12:25 AM
2148	Barstow Valley............"	Lv.	6:25 AM	Lv. 11:45 PM
2229	San Bernardino............."	Ar.	8:50 AM	Lv. 9:20 PM
2240	Riverside (Mission Inn)......."	Ar.	9:30 AM	Lv. 8:45 PM
2259	Ontario..................."	Ar.♦	10:05 AM	Lv.f 8:11 PM
2265	Pomona (Citrus Fruits & Walnuts)"	Ar.♦	10:14 AM	Lv.f 8:00 PM
2292	East Los Angeles.............Cal.	Ar.	11:00 AM	Lv. 7:10 PM
2299	**LOS ANGELES**............"	Ar.	11:30 AM	Lv. 6:35 PM

f—Stops only on signal.   ♦Conditional Stop   Consult Agent or Conductor.
Complete schedules of all Overland Route trains furnished on request.

UNION & NORTH WESTERN RY. 3-15-43
PACIFIC RAILROAD.

The Challenger
Between
Chicago, Omaha and Los Angeles
Time table showing schedule at principal stations

No one knows who yelled, "Well, what are we waiting for?" but the residents of North Platte answered by giving away the cakes, cookies, cigarettes, and magazines to the soldiers on the train. As the giant locomotive came back to life, a father, clutching a $5 bill intended for his son, passed it to a soldier perched in a window. Shouts of "Merry Christmas" and "God Bless" filled the platform until the final rail car disappeared into the horizon.

Company D of the Nebraska National Guard, including
First Lieutenant Denver Wilson, Rae Wilson's brother

Fred C. Peterson
Captain

Dan Craig
First Lieutenant

Dale E. Goodwin
First Lieutenant

Denver Wilson
First Lieutenant

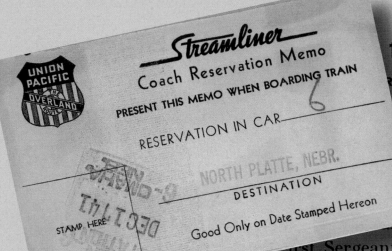

UNION PACIFIC
OVERLAND ROUTE

Streamliner
Coach Reservation Memo

PRESENT THIS MEMO WHEN BOARDING TRAIN

RESERVATION IN CAR _____ 6

NORTH PLATTE, NEBR.
DESTINATION

STAMP HERE   Good Only on Date Stamped Hereon

134TH INFAN

ROBINSON. ARKANS

HISTORY

...ized May 11, 192...

...d Second Lieuten...

...irst Sergeant.   Captain Cool le...

...and was succeeded to command by Lieute...

...enant Land were bo...

...C. Petersen, a Worl...

TOP: Denver Wilson (third from the right), a first lieutenant in Nebraska's National Guard (Company D) and Rae Wilson's brother

LEFT: A train ticket to North Platte aboard The Overland Route.

RIGHT: Welcome arch at the edge of town on the Lincoln Highway

...e first camp ever to...

Aside from learning the art of shoveling, ducking heavy r...
the unit came home as green as it left.   Since that time, ho...
progress in military science

Alford C. Boatsman
First Lieutenant

George M. Seeman
Second Lieutenant

RY

th Captain Cecil Cool,
Robert N. Land as of-
Company soon after
Miltonberger. First
omoted a grade higher
ar veteran, was com-

eld at Camp Ashland.
nd grubbing stumps,
, it has made steady

Rae Wilson, a twenty-five year-old clerk, had hoped to see her brother, the commander of Company D, on that train, but her disappointment soon disappeared. She had an idea that was building like steam in a teakettle, and she had to get it out.

She thought, "What if North Platte could give *every* train full of soldiers, sailors, and marines the same welcome and home cooking?"

11

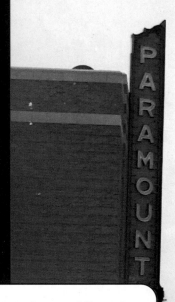

The next day, December 18th, Rae wrote a letter to the editor of the *Daily Bulletin* urging her neighbors to help.

"Why can't we, the people of North Platte and the other towns surrounding our community, start a fund and open a canteen now?"

The war was real, and it was rolling through their town every day. "we can do our part." she appealed, "Let's do something and do it in a hurry."

"We were sort of caught in the middle of the country. There was a war going on one side of us and on the other side of us, our boys were leaving, and here we sat, frustrated. We wanted to do something, too."

—Rose Loncar

Soldiers Canteen Here Is Suggested

Following the visit of the troop train here yesterday afternoon Miss Rae Wilson, sister of North Platte's Captain Denver Wilson, suggested that a canteen be opened here to make the trips of soldiers thru the city more entertaining. She offered her services without charge. Her public-spirited and generous offer is contained in the following communications to The Bulletin:

Editor, The Daily Bulletin:

I don't know just how many people went to meet the trains when the troops went thru our city Wednesday, but those who didn't should have.

To see the spirits and the high morale among those soldiers should certainly put some of us on our feet and make us realize we are really at war. We should help keep this soldier morale at its highest peak. We can do our part.

During World War I the army and navy mothers, or should I say the war mothers, had canteens at our own depot. Why can't we, the people of North Platte and the other towns surrounding our community, start a fund and open a Canteen now? I would be more than willing to give my time without charge and run this canteen.

We who met this troop train which arrived about 5 o'clock were expecting Nebraska boys. Naturally we had candy, cigarettes, etc., but we very willingly gave these things to the Kansas boys.

Smiles, tears and laughter followed. Appreciation showed on over 300 faces An officer told me it was the first time anyone had met their train and that North Platte had helped the boys keep up their spirits.

I say get back of our sons and other mothers' sons 100 per cent. Let's do something and do it in a hurry! We can help this way when we can't help any other way.

—RAE WILSON

The people of North Platte sprang into action, forming committees, donating materials, and baking cookies. Their mission was monumental: to meet every train carrying troops for the duration of the war and to treat the soldiers aboard as their own. Almost three weeks after the attack on Pearl Harbor, North Platte's World War II Canteen began with a handful of volunteers working out of the lobby of the Cody Hotel, right across from the train depot.

Troop trains were loaded for maximum efficiency, not comfort, which made cross-country trips uncomfortable journeys. Anthony Barak described his experience on a troop train, "it was like a cage full of monkeys. You couldn't rest, you couldn't sleep—there was just seating, no beds. It was cold outside as we rolled through Nebraska, but it was so hot in the train. We were supposed to sleep sitting up in our seats or lying down in the aisle."

Traveling soldiers, crowded onto a troop train, head toward their next destination.

16

The first US troops to land in Europe were from the Army's 34th Infantry "Red Bull" Division. More than 4,000 troops sailed from Brooklyn on January 15, 1942, and arrived in Belfast, Northern Ireland, a week and a half later. Most of those troops would find their way to battlefronts in North Africa. At the same time, US forces in the Pacific attacked Japanese forces in the Marshall and Gilbert Islands.

By the end of the war, more than 16 million American men and women would serve in the Armed Forces. Worldwide, more than 100 million troops from more than 50 nations would join the fight.

Rae knew their location wouldn't work for long. Canteen volunteers were exposed to snow and winter winds as they delivered food and gifts to arriving trains. After weeks in the harsh conditions, she learned that William Jeffers, who roamed the streets of North Platte as a boy and was now the president of the Union Pacific Railroad, would be passing through town. When his train arrived, Rae walked up to his private car and knocked on the door, asking Jeffers to use the empty dining room in the depot for their operation. Without blinking an eye, Jeffers consented "Take over tomorrow." and offered to buy cups, plates, and coffee urns for good measure.

Volunteers certainly needed the shelter: winter in North Platte is freezing, windy, and snowy. Summer is often hot, dry, and dusty.

NORTH PLATTE CANTEEN

BACKGROUND: The Canteen register, which details the name, hometown, and date that each service member visited North Platte.

ABOVE LEFT: Rae Wilson, ready to welcome the next train

ABOVE RIGHT: ribbon worn by Canteen volunteers

Having the use of the depot allowed Canteen volunteers to prepare and serve food indoors. Additionally, it allowed for closer proximity to the kitchen and the coffee service area and let workers use tables to serve the food and present magazines and other reading materials. Besides shielding workers and soldiers from wind, rain, snow, and summer sun, the depot also allowed a space for the piano and dancing, albeit for just a song or two. For soldiers, the precious few minutes in North Platte were a time to get off of the train, stretch their legs, and get some fresh air as well as a cup of coffee and a piece of pie. Canteen organizers, who were forever grateful for William Jeffers's generosity, hung his picture featuring his signature cigar and stovepipe hat above the serving tables, as if he were overseeing the entire operation.

TOP RIGHT: Sailor Lloyd Synovec plays the piano for fellow sailors, soldiers, and marines during a stop at the Canteen

BOTTOM LEFT: Margaret McEvoy and Dorothy Loncar welcome a sailor to North Platte with a basket of fresh fruit.

The Canteen Honor Roll

"Red Star Towns"

NORTH PLATTE ★
MAXWELL
BIGNELL
BRADY
GOTHENBURG
COZAD
LEXINGTON
OVERTON
ELM CREEK
FARNAM
HOLDREDGE
STOCKVILLE
EUSTIS
CURTIS
WELLFLEET
DICKENS
WALLACE
ELSIE
MADRID
GRANT
MAYWOOD
HAYS CENTER
GRAINTON
VENANGO
INGHAM
THEDFORD
BROWNLEE
GRAND ISLAND
GURLEY

"Serving Today"

ORLEANS
NICHOLS
HERSHEY
SUTHERLAND
O'FALLONS
PAXTON
ROSCOE
OGALLALA
BRULE
BIG SPRINGS
OVID, COLO.
JULESBURG, COLO.
KIMBALL
SIDNEY
LODGE POLE
CHAPPELL
OSHKOSH
LEWELLEN
LEMOYNE
ARTHUR
KEYSTONE
SARBEN
TRYON
CALLAWAY
OCONTO
ANSELMO
MERNA
STAPLETON

WOW KODY

Prominently displayed high on the depot wall was the Canteen Honor Roll. It was a large board that showed which towns sent folks to work alongside North Platte volunteers on a given day. A red star was placed next to the town name during their shift.

Towns from three states—Nebraska, Colorado, and Kansas—served throughout the war. Many small towns signed up to work one day a month. The remainder of the month, that town's volunteers planned what food to bring, decided who would make the trip to North Platte, and raised money for ingredients and donations.

Ogallala, Nebraska, was the first town to pledge help to North Platte, but soon small farming towns across the Sandhills and beyond added their names to the honor roll. Rose Loncar, whose family served throughout the duration of the Canteen, noted the need for widespread support. She marveled at the resourcefulness of the small towns. "North Platte couldn't have lasted one week by itself. . . . The people from these little towns like Hershey and Maxwell . . . I don't think there are six hundred people in Maxwell, but you'd think there was nine thousand when they came with their baskets of food and stuff."

In addition to food, volunteering towns also collected reading materials to share with troops. Cozad, a small community just down the road from North Platte, arrived one day with over two tons of magazines to distribute.

William Jeffers was fourteen years old when he began working for Union Pacific. He served as a messenger boy, janitor, dispatcher, yardmaster, general manager, and vice president during his fifty-six year career. Having said, "I'd rather be President of the Union Pacific than President of the United States," he got his chance from 1937 to 1946. He had the respect of his employees due to his lifelong devotion to the company and reportedly knew thousands of workers by name. In 1942, President Roosevelt asked him to come to Washington DC to serve as the nation's rubber director. With the natural rubber supply cut off by the war, Jeffers quickly instituted a synthetic rubber program, set the national speed limit at 35 miles per hour, and ordered gasoline rationing. These mandates pushed America to conserve fuel and rubber on the homefront and supply the war industry with synthetic rubber.

The Canteen was run entirely by the women of North Platte and surrounding communities in Nebraska, Colorado, and Kansas. Mothers, aunts, sisters, and daughters banded together to organize, volunteer, and manage the entire operation, which was an enormous feat, all the while still raising families, going to school, and working themselves.

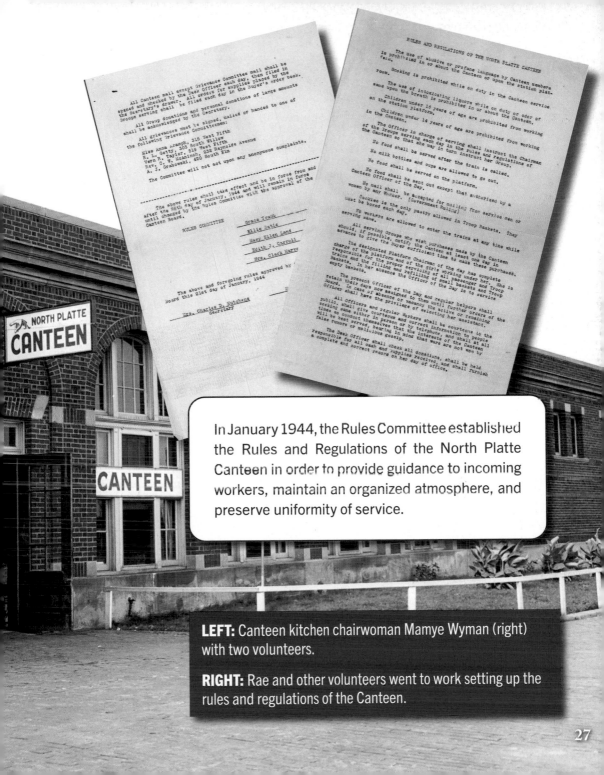

All Canteen mail except Grievance Committee mail shall be opened and checked by the Desk Officer each day, then filed in the Secretary's drawer. All orders for supplies placed by the Groups serving shall be filed each day in the Buyer's order book.

All Group donations and personal donations of large amounts shall be acknowledged by the Secretary.

All grievances must be signed, mailed or handed to one of the following Grievance Committeemen:

Miss Anna Aragon, 315 West Fifth
R. L. Getty, 303 South Willow
Vern R. Taylor, 519 West Fifth
Rev. C. W. McAninch, 232 Reynolds Avenue
A. J. Grabowski, 420 South Elm

The Committee will not act upon any anonymous complaints.

The above rules shall take affect and be in force from and after the 28th day of January, 1944 and will remain in force until changed by the Rules Committee with the approval of the Canteen Board.

RULES COMMITTEE   Grace Traub
                       Ellie Batie
                       Mary Ellen Land
                       Edith J. Carroll
                       Mrs. Clark Harve

The above and foregoing rules approved by
Board this 21st day of January, 1944

Mrs. Charles B. Hutchens
Secretary

RULES AND REGULATIONS OF THE NORTH PLATTE CANTEEN

The use of abusive or profane language by Canteen members is prohibited in or about the Canteen or upon the station platform.

Smoking is prohibited while on duty in the Canteen dining room.

The use of intoxicating liquors while on duty in the Canteen service or upon the breath is prohibited in or about the Canteen, on the station platform.

Children under 16 years of age are prohibited in or about the Canteen.

Children under 14 years of age are prohibited from working in the Canteen.

The Officer in charge of serving shall instruct the Chairman of the Groups serving each day in the rules and regulations of the Canteen so that she may in turn instruct her Group.

No food shall be served after the train is called.

No milk bottles and cups are allowed to go out.

No food shall be served on the platform.

No mail shall be sent out except that authorized by a Canteen Officer of the Day.

Cookies is the only pastry allowed in Troop Baskets. They must be boxed each day. [Government Ruling]

No workers are allowed to enter the trains at any time while serving same.

All serving Groups who wish purchases made by the Canteen should, if possible, notify the Buyer sufficient time in advance to give the Buyer sufficient time to make these purchases.

The designated platform Chairman of the day has complete charge of the platform and of the girls working under her. She is responsible for the proper servicing of all passenger and troop trains and for the filling and refilling of all baskets and troop Baskets. In her absence the Officer of the Day is to service empty baskets.

The present Officer of the Day and regular helpers shall retain their days now assigned to them until further notice. Board. In case of absence or a vacancy the active or order of Officer shall have the privilege of selecting her assistant.

All Officers and regular Workers shall be courteous to the public, shall give everyone seeking information or remaining seeking same either in person and correct information to the times so conduct themselves or by telephone, and shall at all will be best served, bearing in mind that wars are not won by false rumors or malicious gossip.

The Desk Officer shall check all donations, shall be held responsible for all cash and supplies received, and shall furnish a complete and correct record on her day of office.

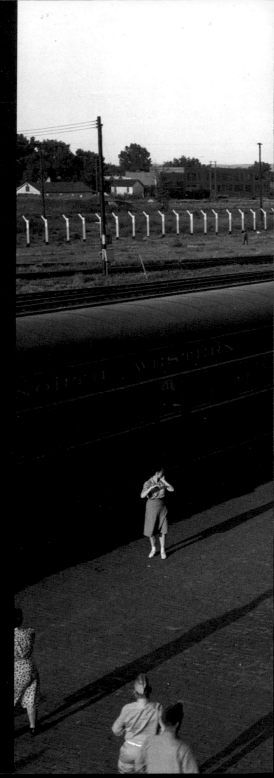

Soldiers, sailors, and marines rushed from the platform into the Canteen to make the most of their brief ten-minute stop. Lorene Huebner, Canteen volunteer, recalls the bustling atmosphere of the Canteen, "The piano in the ballroom at the depot would always be playing when the soldiers would be in and it was so loud . . . but it was wonderful and it gave the boys a sense of home again." Helen Johnson, from Brule, Nebraska, marveled at the pace of the activity, "It all happened in such a flurry, each train . . . you would very quickly start putting out your sandwiches on plates, and pouring drinks so they would be ready . . . There just wasn't time to get to know them. The faces all became a blur by the end of the day . . . I think they were thankful for a few minutes maybe they didn't have to think about the war."

Troop trains were filled with "soda jerks and farm boys, teachers and dentists, students and lawyers, service station attendants, coal miners, iron workers and store clerks who in the prime of their lives were going to war."

—Scott Trostel

Troop trains were a constant presence at the depot. They arrived before sunrise and kept coming well into the night—as many as twenty-three trains a day! When the war began, three thousand to five thousand soldiers passed through the Canteen daily. As the war entered its final year, that number swelled to eight thousand.

This astounding number left the volunteer workers very little time between trains to clean up, restock food supplies and magazines, and brew more coffee. Even though troop train schedules were classified information, the Union Pacific dispatchers would call the Canteen and say "The coffee pot's on!" to alert workers that a train was on the way. Working at this intense pace left volunteers exhausted but also fulfilled and glad to know that they had provided a small taste of home to travel-weary soldiers.

Larry McWilliams, a native of North Platte and a young boy when the war began, recalled that "There were so many trains, with so much soot from the engines, that the soot just became part of the snow on Front Street."

Each volunteer group would send a list of what they planned to bring prior to their volunteer day. This let the Canteen officers know exactly what each volunteer group would be serving. This inventory, from Stockville, Nebraska, was a typical list. Along with oranges, apples, bread, and coffee, they planned to bring "72 [dozen] cupcakes, 37 Birthday cakes, 30 [dozen] doughnuts," and more. The "$151.00" at the end of the list shows the cash donations the folks of Stockville raised and would be donating to the Canteen on their day of service. The money was used to buy more supplies and food, and cover operational expenses.

Stockville

150 lbs Roast Beef	27 Scrap Books
800 Bottles milk	130 Candy Bars
12 Sheet Cakes	145 Sacks pop Corn
3 Crates oranges	1 Pie
5 Bushels apples	1 Puzzle
200 Loaves Bread	75 men & women
5-8 Lbs Coffee	Washed 14 Cars.
8 qts Salad Dressing	
27 Doz Cookies	$151.00
72 Doz Cup Cakes	
37 Birthday Cakes	
30 doz Doughnuts	
13 qts Pickles	
10 qts Cream	
88 doz Hard Boiled Eggs	
73 Packages Cigarettes	
10 decks Playing Cards	
6 lbs Butter	
30 Tea towels	
350 mop	
23 Books	

That $151.00 would equal $2,986.00 today!

N orth Platte started the program, but they needed help, and other towns jumped at the chance. The ladies of St. Luke's Altar Society in Ogallala were the first to help, then groups from Sutherland, Cozad, and dozens of other small towns, some from two hundred miles away, signed up to work a day. After a few months of running the Canteen at a frantic pace, Rae Wilson became ill and was no longer able to continue. Helen Christ stepped in and served as chair of the Canteen until it closed four years later.

Rae Wilson and a team of volunteers (wearing "V" for Victory) prepare the magazine table for the arrival of the next train. Magazines such as *Life*, *Look*, *Reader's Digest*, and *The Saturday Evening Post*, as well as books, puzzles, and playing cards were donated to the Canteen to help the soldiers pass the time on the train.

North Platte was grateful for the help from their neighbors, but greeting soldiers and serving sandwiches was only part of the operation. The Canteen needed money—and needed it quickly. Food prepared in the kitchens across the Nebraska prairie added hometown flavor, but other materials were needed to sustain the mission. Edna Neid bought supplies for the Canteen: sugar and meat from local markets, bread from the bakery, milk from the dairy, matches, fly spray, wax paper, and other necessities. As troop movements increased and America transformed into a nation at war, the cost of running the Canteen escalated. Before officers had to ponder closing the doors, a marvelous thing happened.

As trainloads of soldiers pulled away from the depot and resumed their journey, many sent a postcard home explaining how they were treated during their fleeting stop on the prairie. When moms and dads heard this news, they thanked the Canteen by sending in donations, many of them just a dollar or two. As towns began to work a day at the Canteen, they collected funds to deliver alongside the freshly prepared food. Even President Roosevelt did his part, sending in $5 after hearing the story of the Canteen. These gifts saved the Canteen and allowed it to continue throughout the war while maintaining a remarkable achievement. During the more than four years of operation, the Canteen served over six million servicemen and women and never ran out of money or food.

					45	
Aug 21	Jar					
	Gamble mkt.					10 00 ✓
	Cd. Janitor					1 00
	President Roosevelt's Sec.			5 00		
	Hazel V. Hopkins	Ogallala	Canteen cub.	1 00		
	Victory Cafe	Julesburg	" "	5 00		
	Farmer's State Bank	Big Springs	"	5 00		

The Canteen survived for over fifty-one months without grants or any type of local, state, or federal aid. It depended entirely on monetary and food donations from North Platte and the other 120-plus communities who helped. During 1943, monthly operating costs were $1,000 and later rose to $5,000. President Roosevelt, after hearing about the Canteen, sent in $5 (through his secretary) to support the cause. His donation was part of the $137,884.72 raised during the duration of the Canteen from Christmas Day 1941 through April 1, 1946.

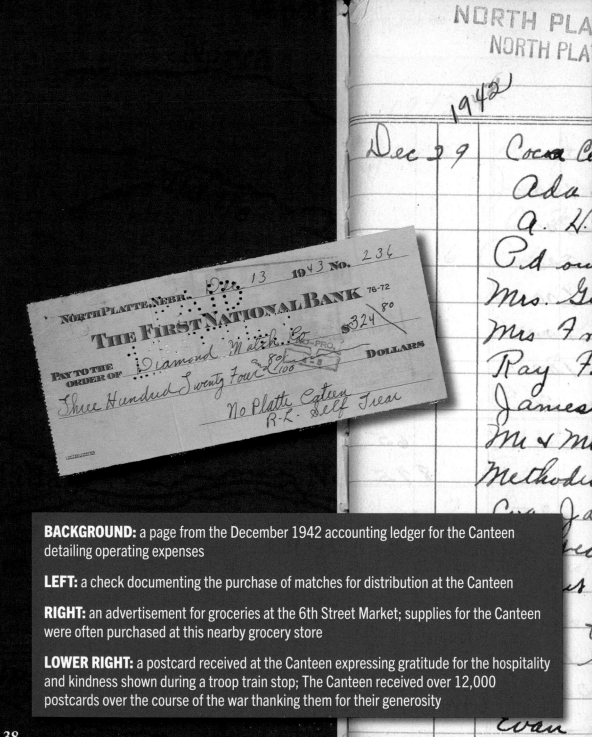

1942

Dec 29

Cocoa C...
Ada...
a. H...
C.A ou...
Mrs. G...
Mrs. Fr...
Ray F...
James...
Mr & Mr...
Methodi...

THE FIRST NATIONAL BANK

NORTH PLATTE, NEBR. Dec 13 1943 No. 236

76-72

PAY TO THE ORDER OF Diamond Match Co. $324 80

Three Hundred Twenty Four 80/100 DOLLARS

No Platte Canteen
R-L. Self Treas

BACKGROUND: a page from the December 1942 accounting ledger for the Canteen detailing operating expenses

LEFT: a check documenting the purchase of matches for distribution at the Canteen

RIGHT: an advertisement for groceries at the 6th Street Market; supplies for the Canteen were often purchased at this nearby grocery store

LOWER RIGHT: a postcard received at the Canteen expressing gratitude for the hospitality and kindness shown during a troop train stop; The Canteen received over 12,000 postcards over the course of the war thanking them for their generosity

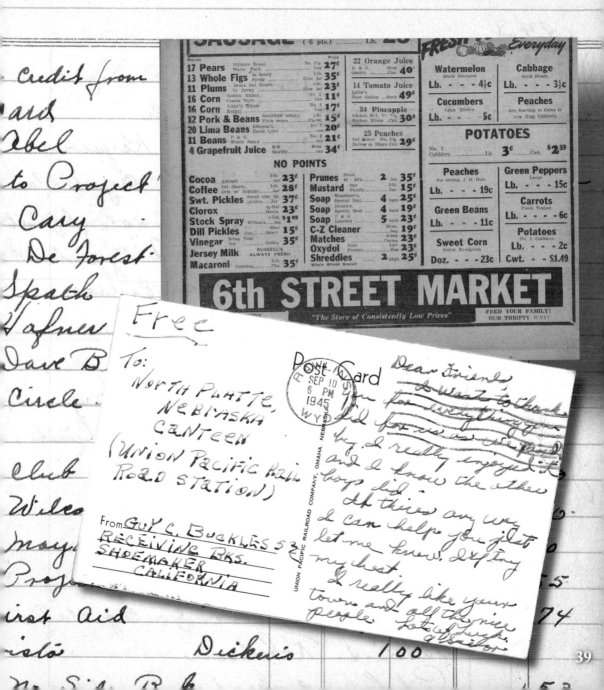

Credit from

ard

bel

to Project

Cary

De Forest

Spath

Hafner

Dave B

Circle

club

Wilco

may

Proj

irst Aid

ists   Dickens   100

SAUSAGE (6 pts.) ───── Lb.

Points		Price	
17	Pears	Hillsdale Brand, Water Pack No. 2½	27c
13	Whole Figs	In honey Syrup 17-oz. Jar	35c
11	Plums	Delsey Del Monte, In Syrup 18-oz. Jar	23c
16	Corn	Golden Valley, Cream Style No. 2	11c
16	Corn	Libby's Whole Kernel No. 2 Can	17c
12	Pork & Beans	Plain sauce 1¼-oz.	15c
20	Lima Beans	Simpson's, Fresh Lima No. 2 Can	20c
11	Beans	P & G Whole Salad No. 2 can	21c
4	Grapefruit Juice	K-R Quality 46-oz.	34c

22	Orange Juice	P & G Quality 46-oz. Can	40c
14	Tomato Juice	Libby's Near Gallon Each	49c
24	Pineapple	Violet, No. 1, No. 2½	23c
	Broken Slices Can	30c
23	Peaches	Del Monte Halves or Slices Can	29c

FRESH Everyday

Watermelon Black Diamond	Lb.	4½c
Cabbage Solid Heads	Lb.	3½c
Cucumbers Long Slicers	Lb.	5c
Peaches Are Starting to Come In now from Colorado		

POTATOES

No. 1 Cobblers ─── Lb. **3c**   Cwt. **$2⁵⁹**

NO POINTS

Cocoa	Aircraft, Del Monte ½-lb.	23c
Coffee	Drip or Regular Jar	28c
Swt. Pickles	Small size Qt. pickles Jar	37c
Clorox	½-Gal Bottle	23c
Stock Spray	Wilson's 1-Gal.	$1⁰⁹
Dill Pickles	Cut Quart	15c
Vinegar	Bring Your Jug Gallon	35c
Jersey Milk	RUSSELL'S ALWAYS FRESH	
Macaroni	Conchas 2-lb. Pkg.	35c

Prunes	Dried, 40 - 50's lb.	2 lbs. 35c
Mustard	Our Family 34-lb. Jar	15c
Soap	Woodbury's, Special Deal	4 bars 25c
Soap	Jergen's, Special Deal	4 bars 19c
Soap	P & G Laundry	5 bars 23c
C-Z Cleaner	28-oz. box	19c
Matches	Carton 6 box	23c
Oxydol	Soap Powder Lge.	23c
Shreddies	Whole Wheat Biscuit	2 pkgs. 25c

Peaches For slicing, J. H. Hale	Lb.	19c
Green Peppers Large	Lb.	15c
Green Beans	Lb.	11c
Carrots Fresh Topped	Lb.	6c
Sweet Corn White Evergreen	Doz.	23c
Potatoes No. 2 Cobblers	Lb.	2c
	Cwt.	$1.49

6th STREET MARKET

"The Store of Consistently Low Prices"

FEED YOUR FAMILY! OUR THRIFTY WAY!

Free

Post Card

SEP 10 6 PM 1945 WYO.

To:
NORTH PLATTE,
NEBRASKA
CANTEEN
(UNION PACIFIC RAIL
ROAD STATION)

From GUY C. BUCKLES 53
RECEIVING BKS.
SHOEMAKER
CALIFORNIA

UNION PACIFIC RAILROAD COMPANY, OMAHA NEBRASKA

Dear Friends,
I want to thank
you for everything you
did for us in the
boy. I really enjoyed it
and I know the other
boys did.

If there is any way
I can help you just
let me know. I'll try
my best.

I really like your
town and all the nice
people. Let us be a
visitor.

The menu changed daily, depending on the season and what community was scheduled to serve. Following the annual pheasant hunt in Stapleton, Nebraska, residents decided to treat soldiers to the local delicacy. Canteen volunteers arrived with dishpans and bushel baskets full of the birds. In short order, stacks of freshly prepared pheasant sandwiches filled the tables alongside jars of the striped tail feathers. Rose Loncar, a Canteen officer, recalled, "it was just like Yankee Doodle Dandy. Every soldier had a feather in his hat when he left. It was something else." In the summertime, Harold Makinson, owner of the Sunshine Dairy, would pull his truck next to the depot and serve milkshakes and ice cream cones until they were gone.

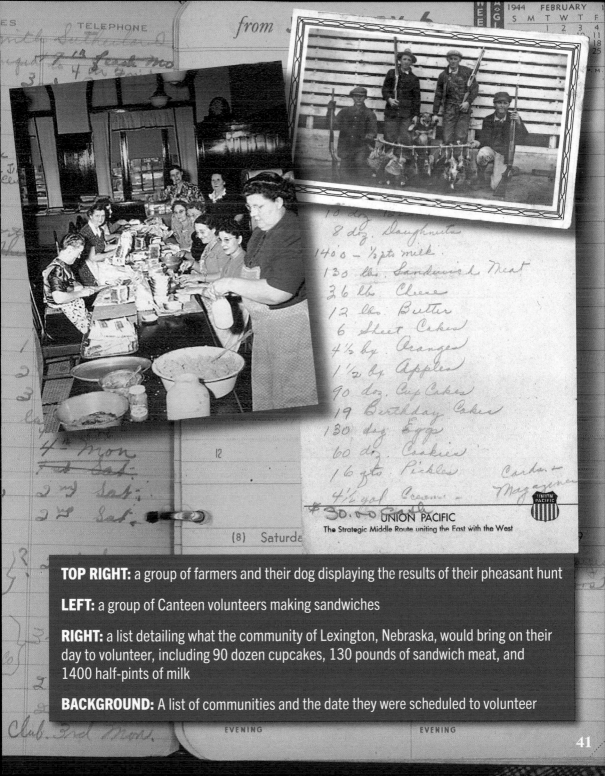

8 doz. Doughnuts
1400 — ½ pts milk
130 lbs. Sandwich Meat
36 lbs. Cheese
12 lbs. Butter
6 Sheet Cakes
4½ bx. Oranges
1½ bx Apples
90 doz. Cup Cakes
19 Birthday Cakes
130 doz Eggs
60 doz. Cookies
16 qts. Pickles
4½ gal Cream
$30.00

UNION PACIFIC
The Strategic Middle Route uniting the East with the West

TOP RIGHT: a group of farmers and their dog displaying the results of their pheasant hunt

LEFT: a group of Canteen volunteers making sandwiches

RIGHT: a list detailing what the community of Lexington, Nebraska, would bring on their day to volunteer, including 90 dozen cupcakes, 130 pounds of sandwich meat, and 1400 half-pints of milk

BACKGROUND: A list of communities and the date they were scheduled to volunteer

George Dawson, a native New Yorker who had never ventured farther west than New Jersey, remembered his brief stop at the Canteen, "It wasn't Times Square, that depot. It wasn't Grand Central Station. But what that depot was . . . I was overwhelmed by the pure, simple generosity. We were treated as if we were their sons. They could not have treated their own sons with more kindness than they treated us." He captured his experience with a short phrase, "There was love there."

Put this
SWANS DOWN

A trio of workers arriving with magazines, napkins, and other supplies for the busy day ahead

To make sure soldiers would have nutritious meals in the field—that were small, lightweight, and didn't require refrigeration—K-Rations were developed in 1941. (They were named for Dr. Ancel Keys, a University of Minnesota public health scientist.) In theory, soldiers would only have to eat K-Rations for a few weeks until hot prepared meals could be served. But unpredictable wartime circumstances often dictated much longer periods of time. K-Rations were sealed in waxed cardboard to keep out moisture. The breakfast K-Ration pictured contained chopped ham and eggs, a fruit bar, biscuits (crackers), a packet of instant coffee, sugar tablets, a small package of cigarettes, chewing gum, water purification tablets, a wooden spoon, and a key (can opener).

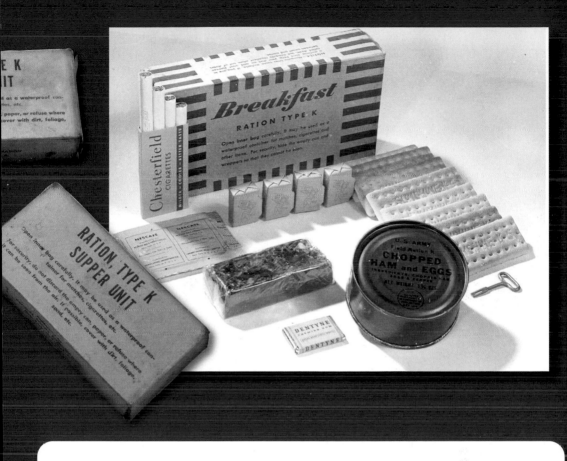

"Some of us were talking, and we realized that none of us will ever forget the lovely, lovely way we were greeted in that place . . . especially after what we had been through. You have to understand, . . . on that train, you had no bunk. You sat up for three days. You had no shower. You were pretty weary. And then . . . you find this unexpected bouquet of nice people."

—Bill Dye, whose ship was sunk by torpedoes in the Coral Sea, described why his stop at the Canteen was so meaningful.

Trains from this era lacked many of the modern conveniences including air-conditioning, ample space for riding and sleeping, and tasty food options. Russ Fay graduated from high school in Milwaukee in June 1944 and was soon on his way to Camp Roberts in California. He described the food in the mess car as, "Pretty soggy . . . the same food every meal. We just sort of accepted it would be that way the whole way." When his train stopped at North Platte he noticed "these women carrying baskets toward our car. It's the daytime, it's hotter than blazes, and we can see that there's sandwiches and things in the baskets." After their stop there, he and the others kept hoping it might happen again, "But it never did—Utah, Nevada, it got pretty desolate, and we'd stop to take on water and coal, but no one ever met us. We never ran into anything like that before, or after." He even recalled reminiscing with other soldiers on the battlefields across Europe about the experience, "We were scraping the bottom of the barrel for food, eating field rations, and someone would say: 'I wish we had some of those sandwiches like they gave us in North Platte.'"

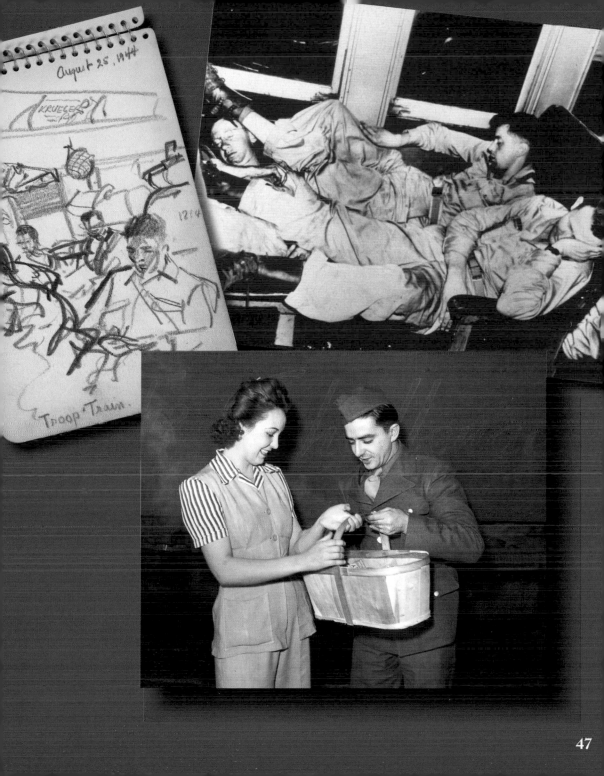

August 25, 1944

KRUEGER

Troop Train.

47

Volunteering at the Canteen—and in other community efforts around the country—wasn't the only job for American women. Many also took full-time jobs in stores and factories that their husbands, brothers, sons, and neighbors left behind. They also filled new jobs that directly helped the war effort: building weapons, aircraft, vehicles, and other equipment. Some women went a step further and joined the military. While women's roles in the armed forces were more limited than they are today, there were still plenty of ways for them to serve their country.

FOREWORD

Hail to the women of America! You have taken up your heritage from the brave women of the past. Just as did the women of other wars, you have taken your positions as soldiers on the Home Front. You have been strengthening your country's defenses—as plane watchers—as flyers—as members of the armed forces—as producers, in war plants and homes—and in Red Cross and Civilian Defense activities. The efforts and accomplishments of women today are boundless!

In 1943 General Mills published a Betty Crocker cookbook meant to help American women do the most with rationed ingredients. The inspirational foreword was meant to energize and inspire women across the country.

Saturday Ni...
North Platt...
March 4 1945

t a day this
t from
ite.

FOR
WOMEN ONLY
OTHERS
KEEP OUT

817½

1 trotting

au to

the fl

called the depot to

was going to be on

e said we weren't

OFFICIAL MEMBERSHIP, DUE AND WORKING CARD
OF THE
INTERNATIONAL
BROTHERHOOD OF FIREMEN AND OILERS
Helpers, Roundhouse and Railroad Shop Laborers
Affiliated with the American Federation of Labor, the
Metal Trades Department, the Railway Employees' De-
partment and the Trades & Labor Congress of Canada

Headquarters Registered No. 252615
CARD OF
Dorothy C. Davis
CLASSED AS A
ADDRESS

Member of Local Union No. 403
of North Platte, Nebr.
DATE INITIATED
3-7-43
DATE REJOINING

INITIATION
STAMP
I. B. of F. & O.
Date 3-7-43

STANNARD-RICKMAN CO., CHICAGO

49

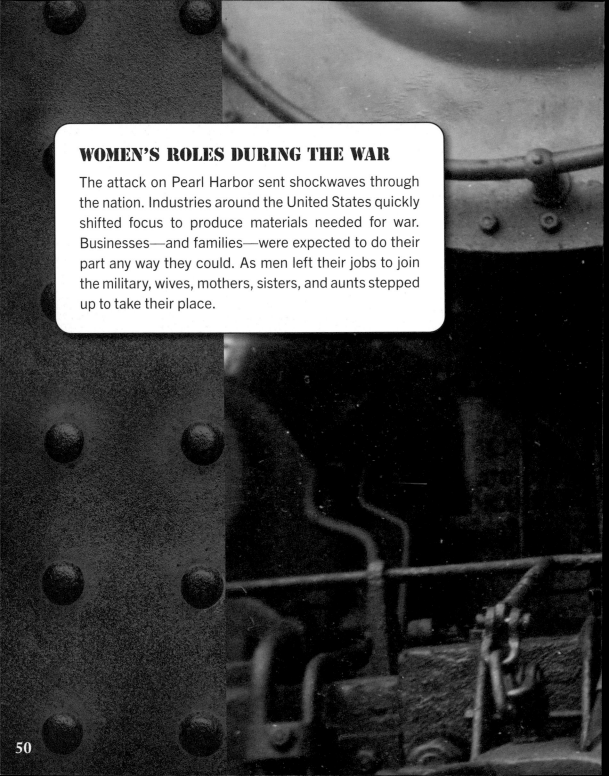

WOMEN'S ROLES DURING THE WAR

The attack on Pearl Harbor sent shockwaves through the nation. Industries around the United States quickly shifted focus to produce materials needed for war. Businesses—and families—were expected to do their part any way they could. As men left their jobs to join the military, wives, mothers, sisters, and aunts stepped up to take their place.

Goldie Johansen, Martha Johansen, and Pauline Jones (left to right) worked at the Union Pacific railyard in North Platte during the war. Often, women would work a full-time job at Union Pacific, volunteer at the Canteen, and take care of the household chores and raise children during the war years.

DEFENSE INDUSTRY

The transformation of the American workforce during World War II was one of the most dramatic in history. As young, able-bodied men left the country by the thousands, young women took their places. And the jobs those young men left changed immediately. Factories that produced washing machines and refrigerators during peace time were now tasked with making parts for military aircraft, tanks, and more.

The Brooklyn Navy Yard (in New York City)—which had opposed hiring women for 141 years—reversed its policy to meet the demands of production. Now with more than 4,000 women workers, the building and repairing of ships could continue. It was a huge change for the whole nation, but also an incredible opportunity. Women who had never had the chance to work could now support themselves. And women who had been in low-paying jobs could now find new jobs that paid higher wages and helped the nation support the war effort.

During the war, American factories produced 297,000 aircraft, 193,000 artillery pieces, 86,000 tanks, and 2,000,000 army trucks, thanks to the sacrifices of six million patriotic hard-working women, many of whom were also raising families and volunteering with community organizations like the Canteen.

Are you a girl with a Star-Spangled heart?

JOIN THE WAC NOW!

THOUSANDS OF ARMY JOBS NEED FILLING!

Women's Army Corps United States Army

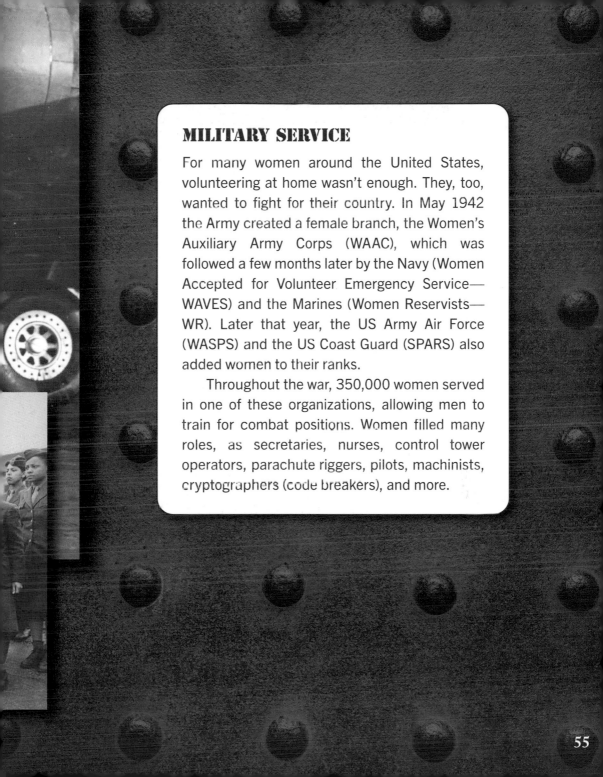

MILITARY SERVICE

For many women around the United States, volunteering at home wasn't enough. They, too, wanted to fight for their country. In May 1942 the Army created a female branch, the Women's Auxiliary Army Corps (WAAC), which was followed a few months later by the Navy (Women Accepted for Volunteer Emergency Service— WAVES) and the Marines (Women Reservists— WR). Later that year, the US Army Air Force (WASPS) and the US Coast Guard (SPARS) also added women to their ranks.

Throughout the war, 350,000 women served in one of these organizations, allowing men to train for combat positions. Women filled many roles, as secretaries, nurses, control tower operators, parachute riggers, pilots, machinists, cryptographers (code breakers), and more.

ELAINE DOMINY

Elaine Dominy was like thousands of other young American women at this time. From the rural community of Tarkington Prairie in Southeast Texas, Elaine was twenty-three years old when she left her job as a shipping clerk at Swift and Company to enlist in the WAAC (later changed to the Women's Army Corps, or WAC). Perhaps she was on a train that passed through North Platte on her way to her remote assignment in the Pacific Ocean.

As a member of the 5203rd WAC detachment, Elaine was responsible for monitoring and enforcing safety regulations within V-Mail communications. Serving in several locations in the Philippines as a staff sergeant, Elaine and her fellow WAC compatriots were recognized for their contributions to the war effort. They earned the Meritorious Unit Plaque Award for their "superior performance of duty" despite the oppressive heat and humidity, torrential rains, and diseases such as malaria and jungle rot (fungal skin infection) that were common in the Philippines. After the war, Elaine's story was not uncommon: she returned home, married another veteran, raised a family, and only mentioned her distinguished service when someone asked.

ATC-PT-43

U. S. ARMY AIR FORCES
AIR TRANSPORT COMMAND
CABIN IDENTIFICATION TAG

Elaine Dominy _S/Sgt_
(PASSENGER'S NAME)   (GRADE OR TITLE)

229   *Leyte*
(TRIP NO. OR PLANE NO.)   (STATION OF ORIGIN)

DO NOT REMOVE FROM PROPERTY UNTIL COMPLETION OF FLIGHT
(SEE REVERSE SIDE)   16-31807-2

AG,
51st
Cent...

GENERAL ORDERS)

NO........157)

APO 500
9 September 1945

MERITORIOUS SERVICE UNIT PLAQUE AWARD

Pursuant to authority contained in Circular No. 345, War Department, dated 23 August 1944, as amended by Circular No. 421, War Department, dated 26 October 1944, a Meritorious Service Unit Plaque is awarded by the Commander-in-Chief, United States Army Forces, Pacific, to the following-named unit:

5203d WOMEN'S ARMY CORPS DETACHMENT. For superior performance of duty in the performance of exceptionally difficult tasks at Port Moresby, New Guinea, from 28 May to 28 November 1944. As the first Women's Army Corps Detachment to serve in New Guinea, this unit was responsible for the enforcement of security regulations in personal mail written by military personnel in the Southwest Pacific Area. Members of the organization censored practically all the foreign-language mail written in the theater, involving a knowledge of 31 languages. Through the skillful and diligent manner in which they carried out their duties, the members ... Corps Detachment contributed ... security in the Southwest Pa...

AG-PA 200.6

By command of Gener...

...ICIAL:

B. M. FITCH,
...rigadier General, U. S. A...
Adjutant General.

DOMESTIC RESPONSIBILITIES

Women who did not join the military or work outside the home were still critical in helping to win the war. Housewives, young mothers, and grandmothers volunteered with the Red Cross, rolled bandages for military hospitals, and greeted soldiers at local USO (United Service Organization) stations. Others enlisted in the Crop Corps, harvesting crops and working on farms across the country.

Many everyday items and ingredients were rationed during the war. That meant every family was only allowed a certain amount of things like sugar, eggs, cotton, beef, etc., per week. With such limited resources, the government asked families to "Use it up—wear it out—make it do, or do without." Clothing was altered to fit growing kids rather than moms shopping for new items. Betty Crocker published a 1943 cookbook aimed at helping housewives prepare nutritious and tasty meals with limited and substituted ingredients. Recipes included Victory Pancakes, Nutburgers, and War-Time Cake.

Women also responded to the government's plea to grow vegetables in their own yards or neighborhoods. These vegetables—grown in so-called Victory Gardens—would feed local communities so commercially grown veggies could go to the soldiers. No doubt thousands of pounds of Victory Garden vegetables made their way to the Canteen.

TOP LEFT: During the war, the government encouraged citizens to plant a garden in order to supplement rations. Roughly twenty million Victory Gardens were planted in vacant lots, public parks, backyards, and on tiny slivers of land in the cities, which produced about forty percent of all the fruits and vegetables consumed by 1945.

TOP RIGHT: Gas ration stickers were placed at the lower right-hand corner of the windshield to inform the service station attendant how much gasoline the driver could purchase. This "B" sticker was distributed mostly to business owners and allowed drivers to purchase eight gallons a week. The most common "A" sticker, issued to the general public, limited car owners to just three gallons of gas a week.

RIGHT: A clipping from the North Platte newspaper explaining what rationed materials could be purchased, the required amount of ration stamps needed, the quantity limit, and the dates the items could be purchased.

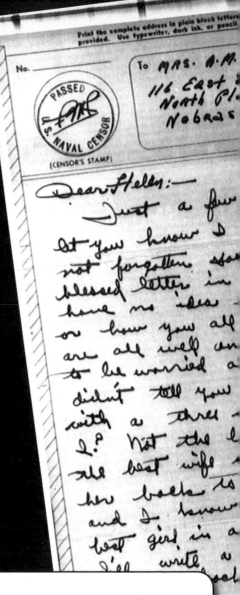

Working a day at the Canteen involved sacrifice as well. Households forfeited homemade pies for weeks, saving the sugar for Canteen desserts. Families walked to work, church, and school to conserve gas for their trip to North Platte. Small towns banded together to make the trip, cooking and baking the day before, meeting in the middle of the night at a familiar farmhouse, and forming a caravan of cars packed with sleepy housewives, tired farmers, and home cooked meals.

"These people spent all that time and donated all that money—to get the sugar and all that stuff. They gave up their own ration stamps. They were using their own ration stamps for us. We all knew what that meant."

—Lawrence W. Jones

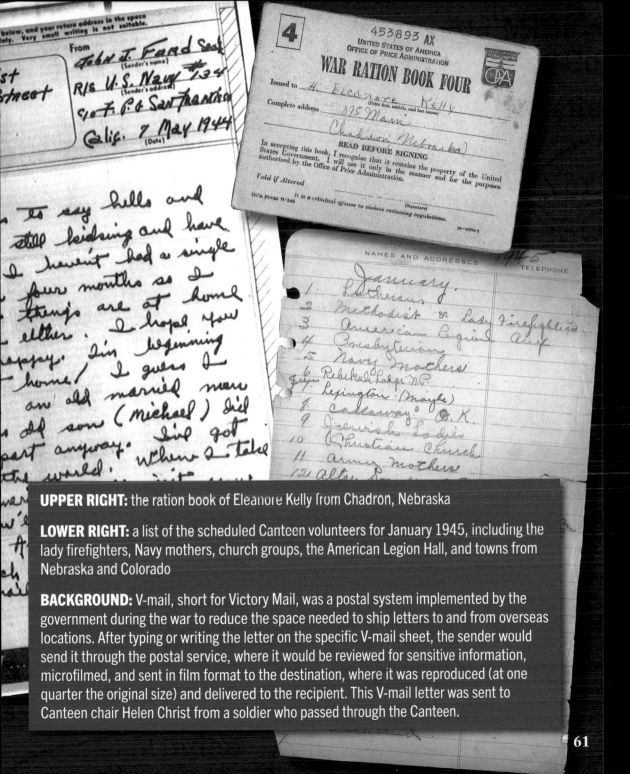

UPPER RIGHT: the ration book of Eleanore Kelly from Chadron, Nebraska

LOWER RIGHT: a list of the scheduled Canteen volunteers for January 1945, including the lady firefighters, Navy mothers, church groups, the American Legion Hall, and towns from Nebraska and Colorado

BACKGROUND: V-mail, short for Victory Mail, was a postal system implemented by the government during the war to reduce the space needed to ship letters to and from overseas locations. After typing or writing the letter on the specific V-mail sheet, the sender would send it through the postal service, where it would be reviewed for sensitive information, microfilmed, and sent in film format to the destination, where it was reproduced (at one quarter the original size) and delivered to the recipient. This V-mail letter was sent to Canteen chair Helen Christ from a soldier who passed through the Canteen.

In August 1944, the community of Amherst, Colorado, made the 220-mile round trip to North Platte. The volunteers from the tiny town arrived at the Canteen with 200 birthday cakes, 96 sheet cakes, 229 dozen eggs, 38 gallons of milk, 50 dozen doughnuts, 4 bushels of apples, 193 dozen cookies, and much more. Forty of the town's sixty-five citizens jammed into eight cars that lumbered along at 35 miles per hour atop bumpy gravel roads for hours—all for the chance to say thank you with a sandwich and a smile.

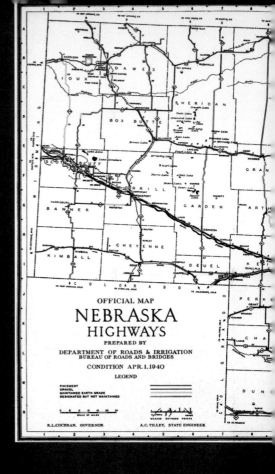

OFFICIAL MAP

NEBRASKA
HIGHWAYS

PREPARED BY

DEPARTMENT OF ROADS & IRRIGATION
BUREAU OF ROADS AND BRIDGES

CONDITION APR. 1, 1940

LEGEND

R.L. COCHRAN, GOVERNOR   A.C. TILLEY, STATE ENGINEER

"I thought what I did for some other mother's son, that perhaps somebody would do for mine."

—Edna Neid

BACKGROUND : an April 1940 Nebraska map showing all of the highways traveled by surrounding towns on their way to volunteer in North Platte

RIGHT: William Jeffers instituted the 35-mile-per-hour Victory speed limit during his term as the rubber director to save fuel and conserve rubber

OURS...to fight for

FREEDOM FROM WANT

At Thanksgiving, the traditional meal with all of the trimmings awaited every soldier who bolted through the doors of the Canteen. One year, Father McDaid, the priest at St. Patrick's Catholic Church in North Platte, provided a dozen turkeys, sixty pies, and other items for a Thanksgiving Day meal. That afternoon, as he sat down to eat his own Thanksgiving meal, a Canteen worker called to inform him all of the turkeys had been eaten. He promptly put his own turkey back into the pan, and rushed it a block away to the depot.

FATHER PATRICK MCDAID, who served in his role from 1910 to 1948, and the St. Patrick's Catholic Church

Canteen workers made special efforts to provide a bit of hometown hospitality to traveling soldiers who would not be gathered around the table with family and friends during the holidays. During the Christmas season, evergreen wreaths filled every window in the depot, a large lighted tree stood in a corner of the serving hall, and every soldier was given a wrapped present during their visit.

"North Platte hasn't any big war industries. Just the railroad running through. But I guess you could say we've started our own war industry—exporting morale."

–Rae Wilson

Christmas Day 1945
Enroute

Citizens of North Platte;

The destination of all in our car
is Ft. Douglas, Utah, or Camp Beal, Calif.
The reason is to accomplish our
greatest ~~pleasure~~ present desire – "to be a
civilian again":

About 98% of us are married and
have at least one off-spring – one
has 5. Most have 3.

Steaming along through Christmas
Eve we all inwardly were hoping
our familys were having a swell
evening and that Santa was generous
to our children.

We went to bed feeling slightly
blue and lonely, not being with them.

Some of us havent caught up
to our pay for two months and
that made even cigarets rather scarce.

But at the stop in North Platte

– 2 –

someone called out = free coffee – free
sandwiches" etc. He just as well
called out "Fire".

Everyone excitedly dressed and
dashed toward the merry
Christmas lights and colors, like
to a water hole in a desert,
– ~~thru~~ under the sign that
read – "Seasons Greetings" – and
into the cheerie friendly crowd
inside.

To have a cup of coffee
in a western town with
friendly western people – to
actually get a present all
carefully wraped from under
a brightly trimmed Christmas
tree, and even the yuletide
aroma that only a Christmas
tree can produce – all blended

The Canteen received
thousands of thank-you letters
from soldiers and their families.

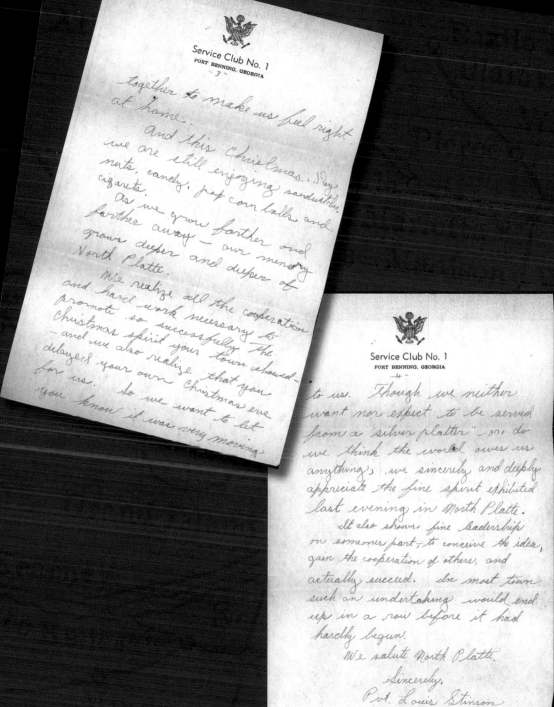

Service Club No. 1
FORT BENNING, GEORGIA
- 3 -

together to make us feel right
at home.

And this Christmas Day
we are still enjoying sandwiches,
nuts, candy, pop corn balls and
cigarets.

As we grow farther and
farther away — our memory
grows deeper and deeper of
North Platte.

We realize all the cooperation
and hard work necessary to
promote so successfully the
Christmas spirit your town showed
— and we also realize that you
delayed your own Christmas eve
for us. So we want to let
you know it was very moving

Service Club No. 1
FORT BENNING, GEORGIA
- 4 -

to us. Though we neither
want nor expect to be served
from a "silver platter", nor do
we think the world owes us
anything, we sincerely and deeply
appreciate the fine spirit exhibited
last evening in North Platte.

It also shows fine leadership
on someone's part, to conceive the idea,
gain the cooperation of others, and
actually succeed. In most towns
such an undertaking would end
up in a row before it had
hardly begun.

We salute North Platte.

Sincerely,
Pvt. Louis Stinson
Sutton, Montana

69

War doesn't care if it's your birthday, but the Canteen did. Platform girls hollered, "Anybody having a birthday?" and soldiers who said "Yeah!" were given a cake on the spot. In March 1945, over seven hundred cakes were distributed to soldiers celebrating their special day.

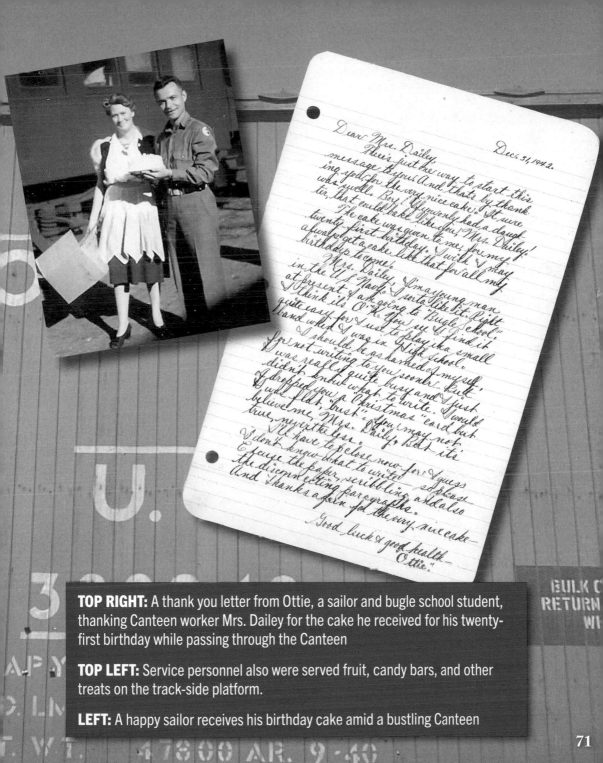

Dear Mrs. Dailey,

Dec. 31, 1942.

This is just the way to start this message to you. And that's by thanking you for the very nice cake. It sure was swell. Boy! If you only had a daughter, that could bake like you, Mrs. Dailey!

The cake was given to me, for my twenty-first birthday. I wish & pray a fun to get a cake, like that for all my birthdays to come.

Mrs. Dailey, I'm a young man in the U.S. Navy. I sorta like it. Right at present I am going to "Bugle School." I think it's O.K. You see I find it quite easy for & us, to play in a small brand when I was in High School.

I should be ashamed of myself, for not writing to you sooner, but didn't know what to write. I would I dropped you a "Christmas" card but was felt "bust." You may not believe me, Mrs. Dailey, But it's true, never the less.

I'll have to close now for & guess I don't know what to write - so please Excuse the paper, scribbling, and also the disconnecting paragraphs.
And thanks a fun for the very nice cake-

Good luck & good health-
Ottie."

TOP RIGHT: A thank you letter from Ottie, a sailor and bugle school student, thanking Canteen worker Mrs. Dailey for the cake he received for his twenty-first birthday while passing through the Canteen

TOP LEFT: Service personnel also were served fruit, candy bars, and other treats on the track-side platform.

LEFT: A happy sailor receives his birthday cake amid a bustling Canteen

71

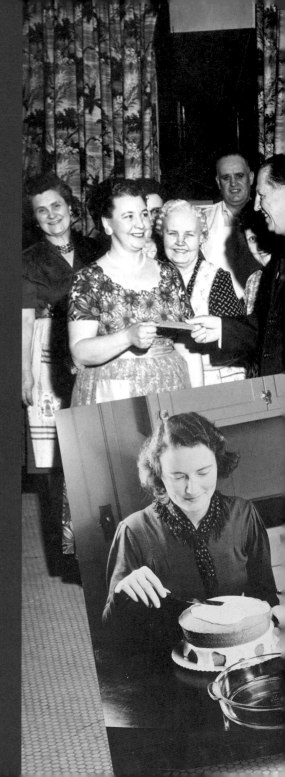

Hazel Pierpoint had been baking since she was eight years old, helping her mother feed boarders in their home. During the war, she made hundreds of angel food cakes for the Canteen, always topping them with "Happy Birthday" in her colorful homemade frosting. She was constantly running low on eggs until her cousin suggested using turkey eggs. The "peewee football" sized eggs went twice as far and were plentiful. Hazel asked her husband to offer a hand by beating the eggs. Before long, he grew tired of that mixing bowl and bought an electric mixer from Montgomery Ward. Hazel soon found out her new appliance wasn't all it was cracked up to be.

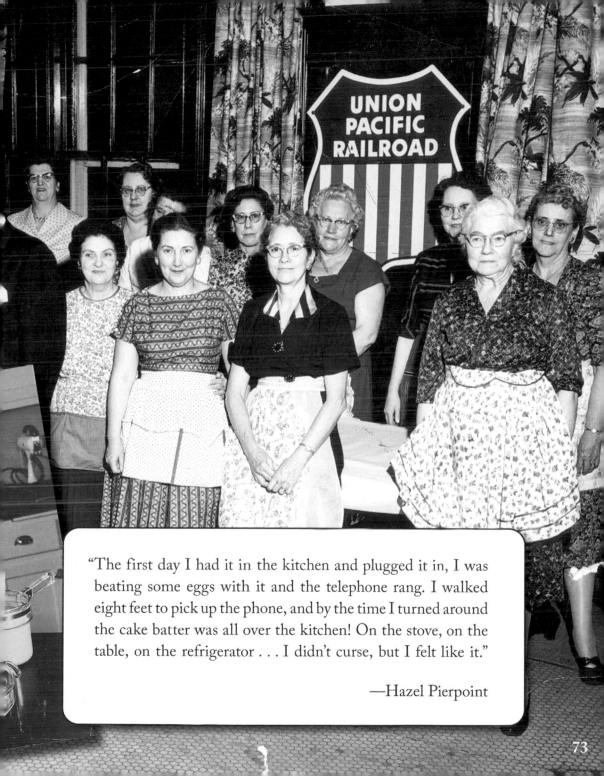

"The first day I had it in the kitchen and plugged it in, I was beating some eggs with it and the telephone rang. I walked eight feet to pick up the phone, and by the time I turned around the cake batter was all over the kitchen! On the stove, on the table, on the refrigerator . . . I didn't curse, but I felt like it."

—Hazel Pierpoint

North Platte Boy Is Honored by Ak-Sar-Ben

One of the outstanding stories to come out of North Platte in recent weeks is that of Master John Eugene "Gene" Slattery, II, the son of a Union Pacific roundhouse worker, who has precipitated the "pro-canteen" sentiment in the North Platte area into donations totaling more than $1,000.

Personable young Slattery's method is to attend auctions, prevail upon the auctioneer to sell something for him, preferably the very shirt off his back. The proceeds then go to the famous North Platte Canteen.

One shirt was sold by young Slattery to Mr. Jeffers for $100, and then the shirt was given back to the lad and he sold it again. In selling 10 shirts, the boy recently reported, he has lost 5.

He also sells anything from goats to a box of candy to raise money for the canteen and January 31 was named a Junior Good Neighbor for Nebraska by Ak-Sar-Ben, which declared he was the champion good neighbor of all Nebraska youngsters outside 4-H clubs.

Such co-operation is typical of all North Platte citizens. Whenever a "good cause" seeks the aid of its people, all North Platte, young and old alike, pitch in to assure its success.

Gene Slattery was a skinny nine-year-old farm boy when the Canteen opened. His older sister had joined the WAVES, inspiring him to "do his part" for the war effort. His chance came when he met a man who was giving away some unruly goats. After putting them inside the fence, he ran inside to tell his mom the news. The goats promptly hopped the fence and destroyed his mother's fruit trees, ensuring a short stay at the Slattery house. Gene knew he could still put the goats to good use. He and his dad took the goats to an auction, and when the bidding started, Gene yelled "I'm giving the money for these goats to the Canteen." Somebody in the crowd shouted back, "What are you going to sell next, your shirt?" And that's what he did.

Gene and his dad drove to livestock sales across the Nebraska and into Colorado, selling his shirts at every stop. The nuns at St. Patrick's School excused him from class and Mr. Hirschfeld, who owned a clothing store, told him, "any time you need a shirt, you come to me." William Jeffers, Union Pacific president and North Platte native, bought a shirt for $100 (that's about $1,700 today!). At a War Bond drive at the Paramount Theater in North Platte, the winning bid for Gene's shirt was $1,700! By the time the war ended, Gene had sold enough shirts to cover the Nebraska Sandhills, raising over $10,000 for the Canteen.

Swede Anderson   Caged   500
L. F. Cain   Canteen Club   100
Gene & Larry Slattery   1745
Miss Chrysta Peden   Canteen Club.   200
Broken cup   05

BACKGROUND: Hirschfeld's Department Store, where Gene received a steady supply of shirts to sell at livestock auctions across the state

The most impressive characteristic of the operation may have been the willingness of workers to make the Canteen open to all uniformed personnel. Women fought for equality and access, even as they were being asked to join the work force and the military. In North Platte, the front doors were open to everyone: troops of all colors and ethnicities, men and women, from all branches of the service, and all ranks were treated to the kindness and hospitality of the Canteen.

Sharing some milk and a few laughs

America during the 1940s was a deeply divided nation, separating citizens based on race in many public places. Black school children attended inferior schools, Black families cheered for their heroes at Negro League baseball games, and families of color across the country were excluded from the best jobs, loans at the bank, and a seat at the lunch counter. The US military also practiced segregation. Black soldiers were faced with the reality of fighting for a nation that treated African American citizens as if they were less skilled, less intelligent, and less important. But the North Platte Canteen and its founders felt differently. They welcomed all military personnel—regardless of the color of their skin—which was astonishing at the time.

When asked about this practice, one Canteen volunteer responded, "Our town, our rules!" then went on to explain they wanted to offer everyone a heartfelt Midwestern thank you for their sacrifice. When asked if this ever caused a problem with other soldiers accustomed to a segregated society she responded, "If they didn't like it, they could stay on the train!"

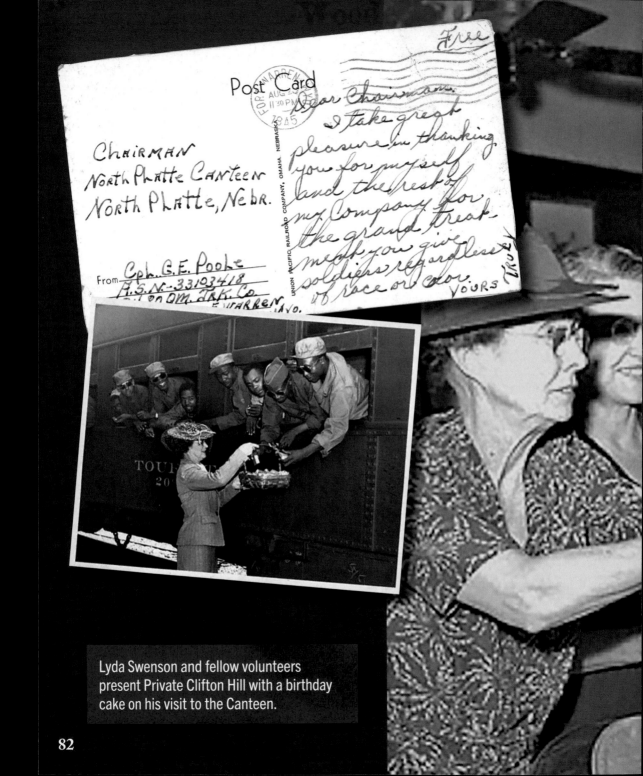

Post Card

Free

Chairman
North Platte Canteen
North Platte, Nebr.

From Cpl. G.E. Poole
A.S.N.-33103418
... on OM. Trk. Co
F. WARREN. WYO.

Dear Chairman.
I take great pleasure in thanking you for myself and the rest of my company for the grand treat. Thank you give soldiers regardless of race or color.
YOURS TRULY

Lyda Swenson and fellow volunteers present Private Clifton Hill with a birthday cake on his visit to the Canteen.

83

August 15, 1945; *The North Platte Daily Bulletin* screamed a two-word headline, WAR ENDS!

Japan had surrendered; the troops were coming home. Downtown was a nonstop celebration. Revelers stood on cars, shouting in jubilation to folks cramming the sidewalks. Businesses closed and churches opened for prayer, both in honor of the momentous occasion.

V-J Day had finally arrived, but the mission was not complete.

Canteen officers knew the troops who passed through the depot would be coming back and pledged to continue until everyone was home. After eight months, they agreed upon a final day.

On April 1, 1946, the ladies group from St. John's Lutheran Church in Gothenburg welcomed the final sixteen trains. The last birthday cake went to Edwin Adams, a sailor returning from the Philippines, his second one! He had passed through the Canteen two years earlier on his birthday en route to the Pacific.

V-J Day, for Victory over Japan Day, was September 2, 1945. The day signaled the end of World War II when Japan surrendered aboard the USS *Missouri* in Tokyo Bay. V-J Day was preceded by V-E Day (Victory in Europe), which ended the war on the European continent with the unconditional surrender of Germany. V-E Day was May 8, 1945.

Rae Wilson returned from California to formally close the Canteen with her successor, Helen Christ. The doors were closed and locked at 5:55 p.m., ending fifty-one continuous months of operation. The next day, three volunteers made one last pot of coffee to drink as they swept and straightened up. During their cleaning, a train stopped at the depot and eleven soldiers filed into the empty dining room. Continuing the Canteen spirit, the ladies stopped working, welcomed the men, and served them the coffee.

RIGHT: Rae Wilson (left) and Helen Christ (right) help take down the Canteen sign while C.H. Land (middle) holds the ladder steady

BOTTOM LEFT: Helen Christ filling the coffee pot

TOP LEFT: Rae Wilson (left) and Helen Christ (right), the two leaders of the Canteen, pose for a picture at the closing in April 1946.

Harry Mulholland, who passed through the Canteen going to and returning from his wartime assignment; "The idea that people had done this—the whole time I had been in the service, that they had been doing it every day and every night at their train station. . . . They were the greatest doggone people."

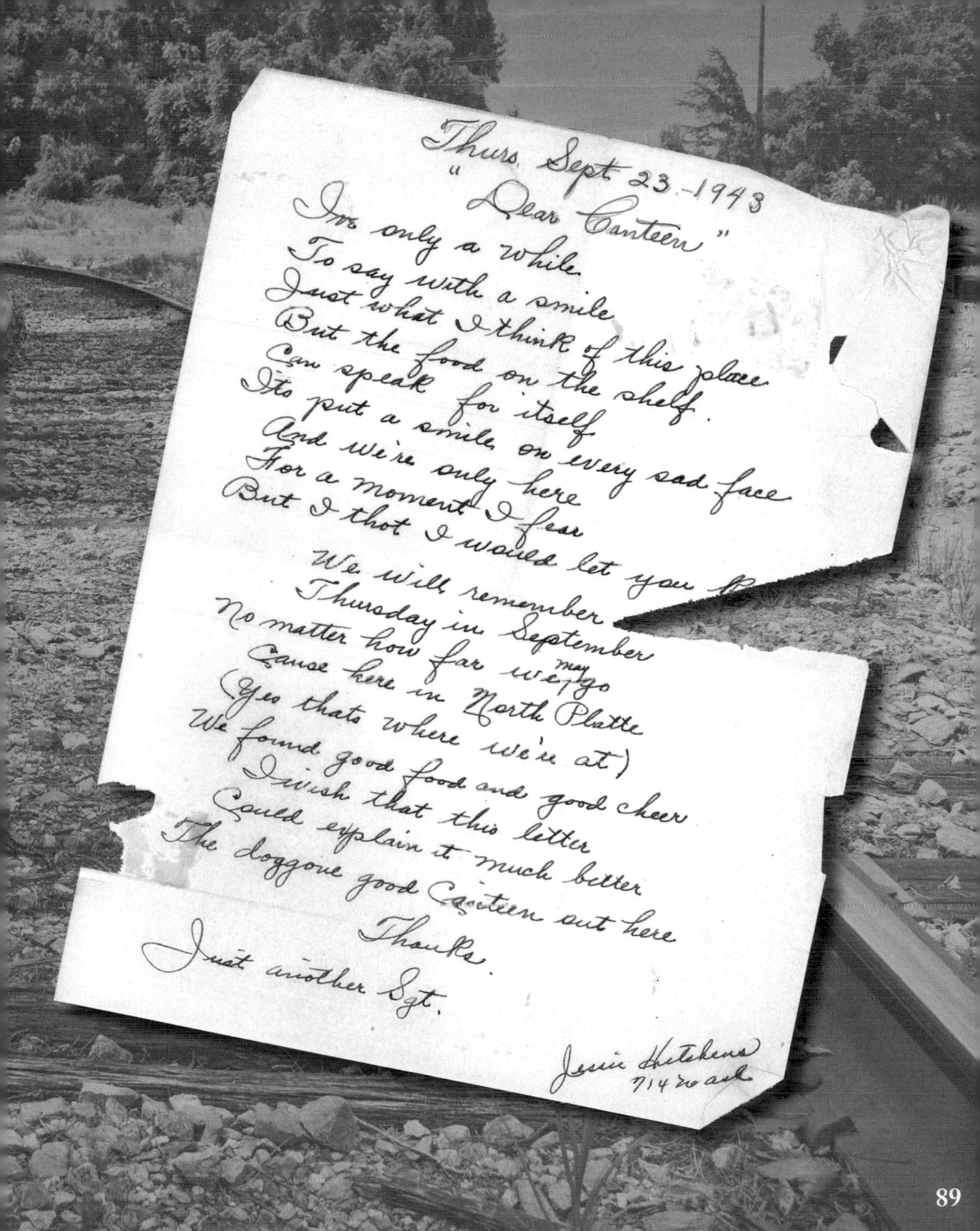

Thurs. Sept 23.-1943

" Dear Canteen "

I'm only a while
To say with a smile
Just what I think of this place
But the food on the shelf.
Can speak for itself
Its put a smile on every sad face
And we're only here
For a moment I fear
But I thot I would let you 𝒦

We will remember
Thursday in September
No matter how far we may go
Cause here in North Platte
(Yes thats where we're at)
We found good food and good cheer
I wish that this letter
Could explain it much better
The doggone good Canteen out here

Thanks.
Just another Sgt.

Jesin Hitchins
714 no ad

"We know you call us 'your boys' but I wonder if you realize whom we saw in you? We saw our mothers, our wives, our sisters and daughters and sweethearts—but above all this, we saw—America."

—*North Platte Telegraph* letter April 3, 1946

Taken in 1943, this publicity photo shows the Canteen officers ready to serve ham sandwiches to the next arriving train. From left to right: Helen Christ, general chair; Mamye Wyman, kitchen chair; Jessie Hutchens, secretary; Edna Neid, supplies buyer; and Opal Smith, platform girls chair.

Timeline

March 15, 1918 •	Union Pacific dedicates the new depot in downtown North Platte on Front Street
July 1918 •	American Red Cross opens a World War I canteen in North Platte at the former train dispatcher's office
September 1, 1939 •	World War II officially begins when Germany invades Poland
December 7, 1941 •	Japan attacks Pearl Harbor
December 8, 1941 •	President Roosevelt delivers the "Day of Infamy" speech. US Congress declares war on Japan
December 17, 1941 •	North Platte citizens gather at the depot hoping to give their Christmas gifts to their friends and families, but the train is carrying soldiers from Kansas, not Nebraska
December 18, 1941 •	Rae Wilson's letter, imploring local citizens to start a local canteen for service personnel, is published in the *North Platte Daily Bulletin*
December 22, 1918 •	A canteen committee is formed with Rae Wilson as chair
December 25, 1941 •	The Canteen opens, temporarily operating out of the Cody Hotel, until Union Pacific president William Jeffers gives his permission to use the dormant lunchroom in the trackside depot
March 1942 •	Helen Christ assumes leadership of the Canteen when Rae Wilson relinquishes her role due to illness
December 19, 1943 •	Canteen awarded the War Department's Meritorious Wartime Service Award. The ceremony is broadcast nationwide on NBC radio
May 8, 1945 •	V-E Day, signaling the end of war in Europe
August 14, 1945 •	President Truman announces the surrender of Japan, ending the war and setting off a nationwide celebration
April 1, 1946 •	Rae Wilson and Helen Christ officially close the World War II North Platte Canteen
May 1, 1971 •	Passenger train service to North Platte discontinued
November 1, 1973 •	Demolition begins on the North Platte Union Pacific train station
July 23, 1975 •	Union Pacific dedicates a marker at the site of the depot commemorating the Canteen volunteers
September 2009 •	*Canteen Lady*, a statue of Rae Wilson Sleight, is dedicated at the 20th Century Veterans' Memorial in North Platte

What happened to...

GENE SLATTERY

Stories about Gene's service appeared in many publications, including the *Saturday Evening Post*. He received the Martin Downey Award for service, a letter of thanks from President Roosevelt, and an autographed photo from Babe Ruth, was recognized for his efforts by Coca-Cola on the "Big Little American" radio program, and even received a birthday cake from Bob Hope.

When the Canteen closed, Rose Loncar and Helen Christ presented a shirt to Gene and told him jokingly, "don't sell it." When the war ended, he started high school, played on the football team, and took over the family farm after his dad passed away. He still lives just down the road from North Platte, growing corn and winter wheat within earshot of the passing trains.

NORTH PLATTE

North Platte has always been a railroad town. Born just after the Civil War as the western endpoint of the Union Pacific line, the modest town grew from a rowdy whistle-stop to a burgeoning community housing the largest rail yard in the world (Bailey Yard). The town claims Buffalo Bill Cody and several other notable Nebraskans but is known across the country as the home of the World War II Canteen. North Platte received the US War Department's Meritorious Wartime Service Award, an honor presented during a nationwide NBC radio program on December 19, 1943, and in 2004, the 108th Congress formally recognized "the outstanding efforts of the individuals and communities involved with the North Platte Canteen to dispense food and good cheer to the approximately 6,000,000 members of the United States Armed Forces who traveled on troop trains" during the war. Although several generations have passed since that time, the spirit of the Canteen lives on in the people of this quaint friendly town. If you're ever in the area, exit from Highway 80 and find your way to the Lincoln County Historical Museum. You'll walk through the same front doors that welcomed millions of sailors, soldiers, and marines to the Union Pacific depot, and you can spend an afternoon imagining what life was like as a Canteen volunteer.

WILLIAM JEFFERS

Born and raised in the Dutch-Irish section of North Platte, Jeffers dedicated his entire adult life to Union Pacific. His career as a railroad man started at fourteen when he quit school after a fistfight with his teacher and took the job as janitor at the local station. Before long, he was a call boy, telegraph operator, and then dispatcher. Known as a fiercely dedicated employee with a fiery disposition, Jeffers steadily rose through the ranks of Union Pacific for forty-seven years until attaining the position of company president in 1937. In addition to helping the Canteen by providing use of the depot and lunchroom, his leadership at Union Pacific helped transform the railroad into an efficient wartime carrier of troops and supplies. President Roosevelt asked him to come to Washington, DC, and facilitate the development of synthetic rubber, a crucial need in the war effort. Jeffers agreed, then imposed a nationwide 35 mile-per-hour speed limit, rationed gas, rankled many politicians and bureaucrats with his hard-nosed blunt style, and moved back to his native Nebraska after successfully completing his assignment within a year. After steering Union Pacific through the war, he retired in 1946 after nearly six decades as an employee. He is buried in Calvary Cemetery in Los Angeles, California.

RAE WILSON

Although the origination of the Canteen was quite serendipitous, someone still had to supply the inspiration and organization to begin the colossal project. Rae Wilson, delighted at the chance to see her brother Denver before he left for war for a few fleeting moments, provided the spark that started it all. She worked diligently, walking downtown streets to ask merchants for donations, calling everyone she knew to bake a few dozen cookies, and approaching William Jeffers in his personal railcar to secure the use of the depot. She maintained the frantic pace, caring for soldiers burned during the attack on Pearl Harbor, often sleeping on wooden depot benches between trains, until her doctor relegated her to bed rest in May 1942. Shortly thereafter, Rae moved to Los Angeles for health reasons. She later married Frank Sleight and had a son, Gary. Rae returned to her native North Platte in 1982 and received the Cody Scout Award from the City of North Platte. Rae died in 1986 and is buried in the North Platte Cemetery. A statue of her entitled *Canteen Lady* was unveiled at the 20th Century Veterans' Memorial in September 2009.

HELEN CHRIST

After Rae Wilson relinquished the reins of the Canteen due to health reasons, Helen Christ agreed to become general chair. Helen was a civic-minded citizen with a gift for leadership and a penchant for hard work, serving in her role for forty-eight months until the last troop train rolled through North Platte. She died in 1956 and is buried in North Platte Cemetery next to her husband, Adam, a Union Pacific engineer.

This volunteer pauses for a picture as she loads her basket with apples for the next trainload of soldiers.

UNION PACIFIC DEPOT

The depot, a stately and vast (80 feet by 263 feet) structure sitting next to the tracks in downtown North Platte, was dedicated on March 20,1918. The building featured red brick, large archways, an expansive area to wait for your train or arriving passengers, and a lunchroom that reportedly served the best meal in town. The depot was a point of pride for local citizens and was often the only part of North Platte travelers might see on the way to their destination. During the war, the depot was in its heyday, bustling with activity. Smells of homemade pies and coffee greeted soldiers as they swung open the grand wooden doors to a room full of surrogate mothers. The piano in the corner competed with the clamor of conversations among invigorated soldiers, grateful for the chance to disembark, stretch their legs, and eat a piece of fried chicken. In the 1950s, Americans increasingly traveled the interstate highway system in favor of riding the rails. Passenger train travel continued to decline until 1971, when Union Pacific decided to discontinue passenger service in North Platte and subsequently demolished the depot in 1973, a decision many citizens lamented for years. Now, a simple monument built with red bricks from the depot marks the spot where the Canteen stood.

Statistics

- By the time it closed in April 1946, 55,000 volunteers from 125 communities in Nebraska, Colorado, and Kansas had kept the Canteen running.

- Over the course of the war, the Canteen received a total of $137,884.72 in donations.

- It cost $1,000 a month to run the Canteen in 1943. By 1945, that jumped to $5,000.

- During the first month of operation, the Canteen was open daily from 6 a.m. until 10 p.m. and served 22,750 troops.

- In 1945, during an average month, the Canteen served 3,350 dozen cookies, 600 dozen cakes, and 600 dozen donuts.

- The depot dining room could comfortably hold 600 people but was often filled with over 1,000 troops and volunteers when two trains arrived at the same time.

- Volunteers brought food onto the trains when a hospital train arrived with wounded troops or when the military police were guarding prisoners of war.

- In one extraordinary thirty-minute period, it was reported that volunteers served about 2,000 troops from four trains.

- North Platte also operated a canteen during World War I. The canteen was run by the American Red Cross and served roughly 113,000 troops during a fourteen-month period.

- An average of twenty birthday cakes were given away each day.

- Troops from multiple countries enjoyed Canteen hospitality, including the UK, China, Russia, the Netherlands, Brazil, Norway, and Morocco.

- Music often filled the Canteen during the day. If someone wasn't playing the piano, the jukebox was playing the latest songs or a local church choir might be performing.

Resources

Casdorph, Paul, D. *Good Times Roll: Life at Home in America During World War II*. New York: Paragon House, 1989.

DeNevi, Don. *America's Fighting Railroads: A World War II Pictorial History*. Missoula, MT: Pictorial Histories Publishing Company, 1996.

Emert, Phyllis Rabin ed. *World War II: On the Homefront* Perspectives on History Series. Carlisle, MA: Discovery Enterprises, 1970.

General Mills Home Service Staff. "Your Share: How to prepare appetizing healthful meals with food available today." Minneapolis, MN: General Mills, 1943.

Greene, Bob. *Once Upon A Town: The Miracle of the North Platte Canteen*. New York: HarperCollins Publishers, 2002.

Hinman, Daisy. "Nebraska Women in the War, in the Service Clubs: The North Platte Canteen." *Nebraska History* 25 (1944): 124–128.

Hurt, Douglas R. *The Great Plains During World War II*. Lincoln: University of Nebraska Press, 2008.

Klein, Maury. *A Call to Arms: Mobilizing America for World War II*. New York: Bloomsbury, 2013.

——— *Union Pacific* Vol. II *1894–1969*. Minneapolis: University of Minnesota Press, 1989.

Kuralt, Charles. *On the Road with Charles Kuralt*. New York, New York: Fawcett Gold Medal Books, 1985.

Lingeman, Richard. *Don't You Know There's a War On?: The American Home Front 1941–1945* 2nd ed. New York: Thunder's Mouth Press, 2003.

Nash, Gerald D. *World War II and the West: Reshaping the Economy*. Lincoln: University of Nebraska Press, 1990.

——— *The American West in the Twentieth Century: A Short History of an Urban Oasis*. Englewood Cliffs, NJ: Prentice Hall, 1973.

Olson, James C. and Naugle, Ronald C. *History of Nebraska*, 3rd ed. Lincoln: University of Nebraska Press, 1997.

O'Neill, William L. *A Democracy at War: America's Fight at Home and Abroad in World War II*. New York: Simon and Schuster Inc., 1993.

Reisdorff, James J. *North Platte Canteen: An Account of Heartland Hospitality Along the Union Pacific Railroad.* David City, NE: South Platte Press, 1986.

Stein, Conrad R. *The Home Front During World War II.* Berkeley Heights, NJ: Enslow Publishers, 2003.

Trostel, Scott D. *Angels at the Station.* Fletcher, OH: Cam-Tech Publishing, 2008.

Uschan, Michael V. *A Cultural History of the United States Through the Decades: The 1940s.* San Diego, CA: Lucent Books Inc., 1999.

Wilcox, Walter W. *The Farmer in the Second World War.* New York: Da Capo Press, 1973.

Winkler, Alan M. *Home Front U.S.A.: America during World War II.* 2nd ed. Wheeling, IL: Harlan Davidson Inc., 2000.

Yellin, Emily. *Our Mothers' War: American Women at Home and at the Front During World War II.* New York: Free Press, 2005.

Young, William H. and Young, Nancy K. *World War II and the Postwar Years in America: A Historical and Cultural Encyclopedia* Vol I and II. Santa Barbara, CA: ABC-CLIO, 2010.

grain elevator in North Platte, next to the railroad yard

Source Notes

3   "We are now in this war . . ." The American Presidency Project (UC Santa Barbara) https://www.presidency.ucsb.edu/documents/fireside-chat-12

12   "Why can't we, the people of North Platte . . ." *The Daily Bulletin* (North Platte, NE) December 18, 1941

12   "We were sort of caught in the middle . . ." Kuralt, 19

14   ". . . it was like a cage full of monkeys . . ." Greene, 217

17   "The first US troops . . ." www.nationalww2museum.org

23   ". . . two tons of magazines . . ." Reisdorff, 19

23   ". . . six hundred people in Maxwell . . ." Kuralt, 20

25   "I'd rather be president . . ." Klein, 506

28   "The piano in the ballroom . . ." Lorene Huebner personal interview

28   "It all happened in such a flurry . . ." Greene, 176

29   Troop trains were filled" Trostel, 10

30   "The coffee pot's on!" Trostel, 65

30   "There were so many trains . . ." Greene, 100

Index

LIFE-LINES to VICTORY

UNION PACIFIC

"KEEP 'EM ROLLING"

THE RAILROADS ARE THE BACKBONE OF OFFENSE

Acknowledgments

A book is a compilation of many things: multiple sources and ideas as well as the mosaic of people you meet along the journey. I would like to recognize the work of previous authors Bob Greene, James Reisdorff, Scott Trostel, Charles Kuralt, and others who captured this episode of American history so eloquently and inspired me to add to the story. My visit to Nebraska in the summer of 2012 was paved by several who extended that acclaimed Midwestern hospitality. Kaycee Anderson, at the North Platte Public Library, answered my questions, helped me track down image sources and bits of information, and was the first to welcome me to North Platte. Jim Griffin, the director and curator at the Lincoln County Historical Museum, opened the vault to me, graciously shared images and other sources, set up interviews with Canteen volunteers, and answered a multitude of questions with patience and kindness, and Steve Kay took an afternoon to share Father Pryor's scrapbooks documenting the Canteen effort and life in North Platte during the war and provided some unique images for the book. Thank you Ann Milton for sharing your insights and images from your remarkable book *Powering Up,* about the women of Union Pacific in North Platte. Bill McGahan took the time to share his local knowledge, discuss Father Patrick McDaid, and also share historical images.

The essence of this story lies within the character of its participants. I was privileged to be welcomed into the homes of several Canteen volunteers and participants and will be forever grateful to hear their stories firsthand. Thank you Rosalie Lippincott, Doris Kugler, Ethel Butolph, Waneita Schomer, Mike Shavlik, Lloyd Synovec, Lorene Huebner, and Gene Slattery.

My colleague at App State, Dr. John Craft, worked tirelessly with me to create the original design and layout of the book, and I am grateful for his friendship and dedication to the project. Thank you to the teachers at Green Valley School and Hardin Park School for reading my book to their classes and offering feedback. Carolyn Yoder was instrumental in the shaping of my manuscript in the early stages, and my friend and fellow author Joyce Hostetter was kind enough to offer support along the way.

I still remember the day my editor Nancy Ellwood called me to say she was interested in this story. Working alongside her and the team from Arcadia Children's Books has been a wonderful ride, and I'll forever be grateful she took a chance on me.

Thank you to my brother Steven, an Army veteran, for sending me Texas-themed care packages and providing much needed comic relief. Much appreciation goes to my mom, Marge. You have always been there for me; now you don't have to keep asking, "When are they going to publish your book?"

My daughter Chandler has grown up hearing this story. She was ten when I started the project, and now she's a college junior and an accomplished artist. Her creativity and compassion for others is an inspiration to me, and I can't wait to see where her talents take her in life.

Finally, I am blessed beyond measure to start and end my days with the most wonderful redhead to walk this earth. Robin, thank you for listening to bits of this story countless times, editing my work, encouraging me to travel to discover a new piece of the story, and for supporting me every step along the way. This book would not have been possible without your guidance and steadfast support. I love you and am grateful for every day with you.

About the Author

Dr. Eric Groce is a professor in the Elementary Education Program at Appalachian State University, where he teaches courses in social studies methods. He has a PhD in educational psychology from Texas A&M University with a cognate in gifted education. Eric is a former elementary grades teacher who taught in Goose Creek Independent School District and College Station Independent School District in Texas. He has served on the Carter G. Woodson Book Award committee and is a two-time member of the NCSS Notable Social Studies

Trade Books for Young People Committee. Additionally, he served as the historical consultant and associate producer for the award-winning movie *Papa Said, "We Should Never Forget"* about the Normandy village of Graignes during the D-Day invasion. He lives in Blowing Rock, North Carolina, with his wife, Robin, and their dogs, Chico and Jackson. He enjoys playing golf, watching the Red Sox and Texas Aggies, and spending time with family.